The Spirit of Faith:

Turning Defeat into Victory & Dreams into Reality

Mark Hankins

The Spirit of Faith:

Turning Defeat into Victory & Dreams into Reality

Mark Hankins

Unless otherwise indicated, all scriptural quotations are from the King James Version

of the Bible.

Quotations of Smith Wigglesworth are taken from "Ever Increasing Faith," Wayne E,

Warner, ed. revised ed. (Springfield, MO: Gospel Publishing House, 1971.)

Some quotations are the author's paraphrase.

The Spirit of Faith

Turning Defeat into Victory and Dreams into Reality

Fifth Edition 2016

Published By

MHM Publications

P.O. Box 12863

Alexandria, LA 71315

www.markhankins.org

Printed in the United States of America.

Table of Contents

"THE LAST OF ALL

HUMAN FREEDOMS

IS THE ABILITY TO CHOOSE

ONE'S OWN ATTITUDE

REGARDLESS OF CIRCUMSTANCES."

-VICTOR FRANKL

1
THE ATTITUDE OF FAITH
CHAPTER ONE

"We having the same spirit of faith, according as it is written, I believed, and therefore have I spoken; we also believe, and therefore speak."
- 2 Corinthians 4:13

I once read a book about a man named Viktor Frankl. Viktor was a Jew in a Nazi concentration camp in World War II. He lived in a flea infested and diseased area. He was constantly badgered, harassed, beaten, and made to carry burdens. Viktor said that in this Nazi concentration camp, he could tell when a person was getting ready to give up and die. He could look into the eyes of those around him and see when their attitudes began to change. He could also see it in their posture as they walked, when hopelessness had taken over their life. Although physically they could have survived and lived longer, mentally they had broken down. Viktor said that he could tell when they were ready to lay down, stop eating, give up and die. He said he could see it in their attitude. Viktor Frankl determined that there was one thing the Nazis could not control in his life; they could not control his attitude. He said, "The last of all human freedoms is the ability to choose one's own attitude regardless of circumstances." In other words, he couldn't control everything, but he could control himself and his attitude.

The spirit of faith affects every area of your life. Paul gives us two necessary ingredients to the spirit of faith – believing and speaking. Believing is the attitude of faith. You can choose fear and doubt, or you can have an attitude of faith.

Even in the middle of adversity, your faith will get you to your destination. God will get you there if you will maintain a spirit of faith. You will have to speak to the mountains and master your attitudes. You may not be able to control what has happened to you in life, but you are able to control your attitude. You have the choice to believe and speak what God says about you. You have the choice to be happy on the way to your divine destiny.

RISE UP IN FAITH

While ministering in Albuquerque, New Mexico, I went to a hot-air balloon festival. This event is the largest hot-air balloon festival in the world. It was an amazing sight with over 700 hot-air balloons flying in the sky at the same time. They had a competition to see which balloon could get closest to the designated target.

A man from the church where I was ministering, actually had a hot-air balloon in the competition and he took me in the balloon with him. Not long after we took off, he told me that we had absolutely no control over the direction of the hot-air balloon. He said the only thing that we had control over was the altitude of the balloon. We noticed that all of the balloons at 1,000 feet were headed south. The problem with that, however, was the target was on the north side of Albuquerque. The man I was riding with pointed out that the balloons that had made it to 3,500 feet were heading north. There was a different wind blowing at 3,500 feet causing the balloons to go a different direction. So we climbed to 3,500 feet and gradually made our way down to the target. The only thing we could control was the altitude. By adjusting that, we made it to our destination.

MOVE UP HIGHER, ANOTHER WIND IS BLOWING

This experience reminds me of people following Jesus and obeying God. Many times you see everyone heading south and you think this is just the way life is. However, if you want to go a different direction and get on the target that God has for you, you are going to have to rise up in the Spirit, rise up in the reality of your redemption, and rise up in faith. If you are living by your feelings and circumstances, you will be flying right at 1,000 feet and you will be headed south. If you will rise up in the spirit, there is another wind blowing that will take you to the divine destiny God has for you.

"FAITH MOVES GOD. FAITH MOVES MOUNTAINS. FAITH WON'T MOVE ANYTHING UNTIL IT MOVES YOU. THE FIRST PART OF YOU THAT YOUR FAITH WILL MOVE IS YOUR MOUTH."

JAMES 2:17-20 // MARK 11:23

2

FULFILLING YOUR DESTINY WITH A SPIRIT OF FAITH
CHAPTER TWO

I once watched a video documentary about salmon. The salmon is known as a fish with a fighting spirit. Noah Webster's 1828 dictionary defines and describes salmon this way, "A fish of the genus Salmon, found in all the northern climates of America, Europe, and Asia, ascending the rivers for spawning in spring, and penetrating to their head streams. It is a remarkably strong fish, and will even leap over considerable falls which lie in the way of its progress."

GOD'S GLOBAL POSITIONING SYSTEM

You may know the story of the salmon as they fight the current to go upstream to lay their eggs before they die. They challenge the strong current, rapids, rocks, and even bears, to reach their destination. Salmon have a remarkable Global Positioning System put in them by God that enables them to travel as much as 2,000 miles to locate the exact stream where they were born. They go up that particular stream, lay their eggs, and fertilize them. Their sense of direction, destiny, and determination is amazing.

The documentary said that there are bears in the streams trying to catch the salmon and end their journey. I found it interesting that the bears are actually after the salmon for their eggs because they like to eat the eggs more than the fish.

DIVINE ASSIGNMENT: THE EGGS YOU CARRY

The remarkable story of the salmon is similar to the life of faith and the fight of faith. The devil is not just trying to stop you; he is after the eggs you are carrying. God has an exact destiny for you. He has given every believer an assignment. When we finish the course God has designed for us and lay the eggs He has given us, our lives are multiplied a million times and reach into the next generation.

God is able to get you in the right place, at the right time with the right people. He has an exact destiny or stream that you should go up to lay your eggs. It takes a spirit of faith to locate this exact stream and overcome the adversity that comes against us as we do the will of God. This sounds similar to the Apostle Paul's life: "For a great door and effectual is opened unto me, and there are many adversaries," 1 Corinthians 16:9. God has a great effectual open door for your life. There is an open door for you but there are also many adversaries. In spite of the adversaries, you can walk through that door and do all of the will of God. Paul did the will of God and left some "eggs" - New Testament letters - Romans, Corinthians, Galatians, Ephesians, Philippians, and Colossians. These letters are still changing lives after 2000 years.

Keep believing and speaking and your faith will guide you into all God has for you. Your faith will open the door of the supernatural for you and many others to travel through. Smith Wigglesworth said, "Never look back if you want the power of God in your life." The spirit of faith goes forward and presses for those things that are ahead.

GOD'S OSCARS FOR ACTORS OF FAITH

The spirit of faith is necessary to do the will of God and finish the course He has for you. God wants you to finish your course, keep the faith, serve your generation according to the will of God, and finish with joy (2 Timothy 4:7, Acts 13:36).

The spirit of faith has an attitude and an action. Believing is the attitude and speaking is the action. When we keep our speaker connected to our believer, the spirit of faith carries us to our divine destiny.

Hebrews 11 lists some heroes of faith. The phrase "by faith" is used 20 times in reference to men and women who did the will of God. They received the promises of God in their generation and they are influencing the lives of millions of believers even today.

The Message Bible translates the phrase "by faith" as "by an act of faith." Faith is an act. Act like Jesus has done what He said He did. Act like you would if you already had the thing you are believing God for. Act like you are who He says you are. Act like you can do what God says you can do. Remember, faith is an act.

Hebrews 11 contains some of God's greatest actors. God gave Oscars to these heroes of faith. Roll out the red carpet and get the camera ready. It is time for some more actors and the awards are eternal!

"FAITH PLEASES GOD.

IT IS IMPOSSIBLE

TO PLEASE GOD

AND NOT KNOW IT."

HEBREWS 11:6

3

TRAJECTORY OF FAITH

CHAPTER THREE

One day, I watched a championship golf match on television. One of the greatest golfers in the world stood on the green needing to make a very critical putt. Millions of people watched with millions of dollars at stake.

The golfer walked around on the green and viewed the location of the ball from several different angles. He carefully prepared to putt as the crowd watched almost breathlessly. When he hit the ball, it looked like he putted the wrong way! It looked as though he had misjudged the putt and the ball was off course.

Amazingly, the ball turned and headed right into the hole. As the crowd cheered, I sat there amazed that he had made the putt. I thought he had putted the ball the wrong way. However, from my view, I could not see the lay of the land on the green. The golfer actually had to putt the ball uphill because the direction and pace of the ball were critical. He judged it perfectly and the ball landed right in the hole.

FAITH WILL GET YOU
TO YOUR DESTINATION

As I thought about this, the Lord spoke to me, "I am a champion at 'putting' people in the right direction with the perfect pace so that they can fulfill their destiny. When you think I am 'putting' you the wrong way, remember, I can see the lay of the land. I know your strengths and weaknesses. I will perfect that which concerns you," Psalm 138:8.

Every man or woman in Christ has a definite trajectory of faith and destiny. When it looks like God is "putting" you the wrong way, remember – He is a champion. He is able by His Spirit to get you in the right place at the right time to fulfill the call of God on your life.

FAITH GETS HAPPY NOW

When you look at the life of the Apostle Paul, you will see a man that God had perfectly "putted" to a divine calling and destiny. You can see the genius of God as you see the many turning points in the trajectory of Paul's life. You can also see the spirit of faith working to overcome adversity. Paul had been stoned, shipwrecked, snake-bit, beat in the head, and left for dead. He could have said he was a tired, mistreated, lonely, disappointed, and hurting man. If you consider the adversity Paul encountered in his life, you would expect him to say something like that. Instead, Paul described himself as a happy man.

The joy of Jesus strengthened the Apostle Paul through all adversity. Paul's assignment was to assemble the thoughts given to him by Jesus and to publish the message throughout the body of Christ. God used him as a mouthpiece to speak and write to believers in every generation. In Philippians, one of his last letters, Paul speaks of joy and rejoicing sixteen times in four short chapters. Towards the end of his life, Paul stood before the leaders of the Roman Empire and said, "I think myself happy," Acts 26:2. Another translation says, "I have been congratulating myself, King Agrippa."

"...so that I might finish my course with joy..."
- *Acts 20:24*

Paul's spirit of faith carried him to his divine destination. He finished his course with joy and completed the assignment given to him by Jesus Christ. He enjoyed the journey in spite of all the adversity he faced. Faith gets happy now!

THE KING STILL HAS ONE MORE MOVE

If you have ever been to Europe, especially France, you know that they have all kinds of art displays. I heard the story of a group that was touring the artwork at the Louvre. In that group was an international chess champion. The group was going through the Louvre looking at the artwork when they came to a picture that was titled, "Checkmate." The international chess champion was especially interested in this piece of artwork. The artist had drawn a chessboard where it looked like the king had no more moves. The picture showed the chess player with his head in his hands and the devil laughing at him.

The group looked at the picture and moved on; but the chess champion stayed at the picture and stared at it. After a while, the leader of the group came back to check on him. The international chess champion said, "You know, they're either going to have to change the name of this picture or change the picture, because I am an expert and I can see that the king still has one more move."

This is also true of believers. Many of them have their heads down. The devil is laughing at them and it looks like it's all over. However, God wants you to know that you are going to have to change the name of the picture because the King has one more move! As you maintain a spirit of faith and let God make His move, the picture will reverse. Now the devil has his head down and you are the one that is laughing!

"ANYTIME GOD WANTS

TO CHANGE SOMEONE'S LIFE,

HE ALWAYS TOUCHES

THEIR MOUTH."

JEREMIAH 1:1-12 // JOSHUA 1:8

4

CAN YOU HEAR THIS...
CHAPTER FOUR

Long lines of jobless Americans were a common sight in the larger cities during the Great Depression here in the United States. Long periods of unemployment had caused many to lose faith in themselves and in their future. Feeling angry and humiliated, many were living on charity.

One of my favorite stories happened during this period in our nation's history about an employer who announced he had one job available. As the word got out, a long line of applicants formed outside his office for an interview and a chance at employment. His secretary showed applicants into the boss' office one at a time.

During the middle of the process, one man ran from the back of the line, passed the secretary, and right into the boss' office. In a few minutes, the boss came out with the man and announced to the others waiting in line that they could go home, because this man had the job. Many began to complain how unfair it was that the man had not waited his turn.

The boss explained that during the interview process, he had thought of a quicker way to select the best person for the job. Because he needed someone who could understand Morse Code, he tapped out so that everyone could hear, "If you can hear this, jump up now and run into my office. You have the job." All the men and women in line heard the tapping, but it did not mean anything to them; however, it changed the life of this new employee.

EVERYBODY — ANYBODY — SOMEBODY

Faith begins with hearing a certain sound that other people cannot hear.

> "So then faith cometh by hearing, and hearing by the
> word of God. But I say, Have they not heard? Yes
> verily, their sound went into all the earth, and their
> words unto the end of the world." - Romans 10:17,18

I like this definition of whosoever: everybody won't, anybody can, but somebody will. Jesus continually used the word whosoever.

> *"If any man have ears to hear, let him hear. And he*
> *said unto them, Take heed what ye hear: with what*
> *measure ye mete, it shall be measured to you; and*
> *unto you that hear shall more be given. For he that*
> *hath, to him shall be given; and he that hath not,*
> *from him shall be taken even that which he hath."*
> *- Mark 4:23-25*

Our hearing has a lot to do with our having. Some have said that there are two groups of people: the haves and the have nots. Jesus also implied that there are two groups of people: the hearers and the hear nots (that isn't good English, but you know what I mean). Faith comes by hearing a certain sound. Faith comes by hearing the Word of God. The Word of God opens our ears to the supernatural plan and provision of God.

THE SOUND OF ABUNDANCE

In 1 Kings 18, after a 31/2 year drought, the prophet Elijah said, "There is a sound of abundance of rain." Elijah began to pray on the top of Mount Carmel when there was not a cloud in sight. He prayed persistently until a cloud about the size of a man's hand appeared. When the small cloud appeared, Elijah outran the king's chariot as the "abundance of rain" fell and brought new life to the land.

Elijah's faith began by hearing the sound of the "abundance of rain." No one else could hear anything, but Elijah was hearing from heaven. As he prayed, his faith became sight and substance. But he got it on the inside before he got it on the outside.

The voice of the Lord is upon the people today in every nation! God is looking for people who can hear the sound of His voice and follow His plan and purpose. This sound always brings the supernatural power of God. This sound will get us praying like Elijah prayed. Elijah prayed with persistence and expectation. He knew it was God's will and the manifestation must come. There is a sound of salvation, healing, deliverance, and blessing in the Gospel of Christ.

The spirit of faith hears, believes, and speaks the same sound. The spirit of faith can be heard and seen. Faith acts on the Word of God; it acts like the Bible is true. Today, the Spirit of God is saying, "If you can hear this, jump up now and run into my office. You have the job."

The spirit of faith also requires a positive attitude.

A person cannot be negative, critical, and constantly complaining and claim to have a spirit of faith.

I heard the story about a man who was asleep in his bedroom and some friends played a joke on him. While he was sleeping, they wiped a piece of Limburger cheese under his nose. Immediately, the man woke up and exclaimed, "Man it sure stinks in here!" He walked out of his bedroom into the living room and said, "It stinks in here!" Then he walked into the kitchen and said, "It stinks in here!" He went out the front door, looked up at the sky, breathed in deeply, and said, "The whole world stinks!"

The lesson from this story is that anytime it stinks everywhere you go, the stink is underneath your nose. You are carrying the stink with you.

Some people are negative and critical all the time and think there is something wrong with everyone else when they are the ones who have the problem. A negative, critical attitude is not a spirit of faith.

You can take the Word of God and clean under your nose or clean your mind. As you meditate on the Word, your mind is renewed, and your attitude changes. Then everywhere you go you can smell victory! Paul faced many tough problems, but he said, "It smells like victory to me." He had a spirit of faith.

"Now thanks be unto God, which always causeth us to triumph in Christ, and maketh manifest the savour [smell] of his knowledge by us in every place." - 2 Corinthians 2:14

GOD'S WORD IN YOUR MOUTH

IS SUPERNATUAL

"MOUTH-TO-MOUTH"

RESUSCITATION.

2 TIMOTHY 3:16

5

YOUR MOUNTAIN NEEDS TO HEAR YOUR VOICE

CHAPTER FIVE

God had some great, glorious, marvelous, wonderful things prepared for me that were being blocked. One day while I was praying and studying, the Holy Spirit began to give me a vision of the possibilities of things God wanted to do in my life; but there were some "mountains" between God's best blessings and me. He said, "If you knew what was on the other side of your mountain, you would move it!" Mountains were hindering or blocking the blessings of God in my life.

To motivate me to use my faith, the Holy Spirit said again and again, "If you knew what was on the other side of your mountain, you would move it!" As I looked at Mark 11:23 over and over again, I began to get a clearer understanding of what Jesus was saying:

"For verily I say unto you, That whosoever shall say unto this mountain, Be thou removed, and be thou cast into the sea; and shall not doubt in his heart, but shall believe that those things which he saith shall come to pass; he shall have whatsoever he saith." - Mark 11:23

"And the Lord said, If ye had faith as a grain of mustard seed, ye might say unto this sycamine tree, Be thou plucked up by the root, and be thou planted in the sea; and it should obey you." - Luke 17:6

In this scripture, the illustration is a "sycamine tree." Someone once joked, "I have identified my problem, and I am sick of mine." Sometimes things will stay around until you get sick and tired of being sick and tired, and you determine that things must change in your life. Here Jesus uses the illustration of a tree, because moving a tree requires dealing with roots that have been there for a long time. The tree and its roots could represent a variety of problems in your life.

I like what Smith Wigglesworth said in the book, ***Ever Increasing Faith***: "Any man may be changed by faith no matter how he may be fettered." In Mark 11:23, you can see that Jesus said this kind of faith will work for "whosoever," and it will work on "whatsoever." In other words, this will work for anyone on anything!

Notice exactly the way that Jesus stated this in Luke 17:6: "...say unto this sycamine tree, Be thou plucked up by the root, and be thou planted in the sea; and it should obey you." Jesus did not say it would obey your favorite anointed preacher, it will obey you! He did not even say that it would obey God. Jesus said that it should obey you!

When you put this with Mark 11:23, "...whosoever shall say unto this mountain...he shall have whatsoever he saith," you can see the power of faith-filled words.

You can see that it is not up to God or someone else to deal with the situation. Your mountain will obey you! Your mountain needs to hear your voice!

Jesus did not say to talk to God about the problem; He told you to speak to the problem yourself. After all, it is your mountain or tree or problem, and it is in the way of supernatural increase and blessing in your life. Your mountain needs to hear your voice.

You may be waiting on God, but God is really waiting on you! Often we miss it when we don't examine the scriptures closely enough. Your mountain needs to hear your voice! You can make it personal right now and say, "My mountain needs to hear my voice!"

YOUR VOICE IS YOUR ADDRESS IN THE SPIRIT

What is there about your voice that is so important? Why did Jesus say, "...he shall have whatsoever he saith"? First, there is no other voice like your voice. Your voice is your address in the realm of the spirit. Scientists tell us that the voice-print is just as accurate in determining an individual's identity as their fingerprint. They say there is no other voice like your voice. In certain high security situations, a person must speak, and his voice must be recognized before clearance is given.

> *"In my distress I called upon the Lord, and cried unto my God: he heard my voice out of his temple, and my cry came before him, even into his ears. Then the earth shook and trembled; the foundations of the hills moved..." - Psalm 18:6, 7*

It doesn't take long for your voice to reach heaven and enter the ears of Almighty God. He is the source of your authority as a believer. Heaven responds to your voice. If your voice moves heaven, you know it moves mountains and trees. This is the way to have a change of scenery in your life. You must lift up your voice with the voice of faith that believes, expects, and will not be denied.

E.W. Kenyon said, "The reason the majority of Christians are weak, though they are earnest, is because they have never dared to make a confession of who they are in Christ."

Not only does God respond to the voice of faith, but angels are also activated by your words. An angel told Daniel, "...thy words were heard, and I am come for thy words," Daniel 10:12. Daniel's words brought the answer from heaven, and the angel came to exactly the right address!

Ruth Ward Heflin points out in her book, Glory, that the word "ladder" in the Old Testament, when Jacob saw angels ascending and descending (Genesis 28:12), has the same numerical value as the word "voice" in the New Testament.

Is it possible that angels travel on your "voice ladder"? Your voice is the highway that angels travel on to bring things to you from heaven. Traffic could be blocked right now if you are not saying much. God needs you to believe and speak. He needs you to lift your voice in faith for His power to be released at the point of your need. This is one of the reasons why you should lift your voice more in praise and faith to God.

IF THERE IS A MOUNTAIN IN YOUR WAY, "QUARK IT"

Sometime ago I saw an article in Time magazine that caught my attention. The article, "What's Hiding in the Quarks," tells how the discovery of quarks were made at the giant Tevatron accelerator at the Fermi National Accelerator Laboratory near Chicago.

The evidence came from collisions between subatomic protons and anti-protons at very high speeds. Not only were quarks discovered, but the Tevatron is so powerful it can investigate the structure of the quarks themselves. What are quarks made of? What is hiding in the quarks? The article states:

> *Physicists were understandably overjoyed in 1994 when they discovered the top quark. At last after 17 years of searching, they had found the sixth — and, according to the theorists, the last — of matter's tiniest, most fundamental building blocks. The*

most troublesome loose end in the so-called Standard Model of particle physics had been tidied up. Or so they thought. According to a report in the current Science, the same people who discovered the top quark may have inadvertently made a much more revolutionary discovery. Contrary to what physicists have believed for the past 30 years, quarks may not be the most basic units of matter after all.

There is something smaller than the atom and the proton. All matter is made of this secret substance. The answer helps us see the origin of all things. The answer could be what many scientists believe today: Quarks are made of sound waves.

I believe this is the answer because that is what the Bible teaches. The tiniest building block of all things is sound waves. Over and over it says in Genesis, "and God said."

> *"And God said, Let there be light: and there was light." - Genesis 1:3*

You can clearly see that God created everything with His voice. He spoke the worlds into existence. You can also see that things created with words can also be dismantled or dissolved with words.

> *"By the word of the Lord were the heavens made; and all the host of them by the breath of his mouth... For he spake, and it was done; he commanded, and it stood fast." - Psalm 33:6, 9*

Jesus described the power of the God-kind of faith in Mark 11:23. The example He gave the disciples when He cursed the fig tree was not a "deity trick" reserved for the Godhead. Jesus said, "Whosoever shall say...."

Another Biblical example that quarks are made of sound waves is found in this scripture:

> *"Through faith we understand that the worlds were framed by the word of God, so that things which are seen were not made of things which do appear." - Hebrews 11:3*

The worlds were framed by the Word of God. This great faith chapter in the Bible takes us back before Abraham's faith to the God-kind of faith that was used in creation. Abraham had to catch the spirit of faith before the miracle that God had promised him could be performed.

> *"(As it is written, I have made thee a father of many nations,) before him whom he believed, even God, who quickeneth the dead and calleth those things which be not as though they were." - Romans 4:17*

THE WORDS SPOKEN TO YOU MUST BE SPOKEN THROUGH YOU

God calls things which be not as though they were. God calls things. Abraham had to agree with God before the miracle could come to pass. The Word spoken to you must be spoken through you.

Dr. Lilian B. Yeomans said it this way, "God has tied himself irrevocably to human cooperation in the execution of divine purposes. He has made man's faith a determining factor in the work of redemption." God is looking for someone to believe Him and say the same thing.

Faith is the substance — the substance that everything is made of is faith.

> *"Now faith is the substance of things hoped for, the evidence of things not seen." - Hebrews 11:1*

> *"Now faith is the assurance (the confirmation, the title-deed) of the things [we] hope for, being the proof of things [we] do not see and the conviction of their reality — faith perceiving as real fact what is not revealed to the senses." - Hebrews 11:1, Amplified Bible*

The Cotton Patch translation says, "Now faith is the turning of dreams into deeds; it is betting your life on unseen realities." Faith always comes with a sound, a voice, and a word. The visible was made from the invisible. Things that are seen are not made of things that can be seen. The unseen is more powerful than the seen. That is why we walk by faith and not by sight (2 Corinthians 5:7).

Hiding in the quarks is the voice of faith that frames our world. The spirit of faith contains the building blocks of the will of God in our lives. All the redemptive rights and privileges that belong to us in Christ must be appropriated by faith. The authority of the believer is released through the words that move mountains and trees and make demons flee.

WHOSOEVER SHALL HAVE WHATSOEVER

In Mark 11:23, Jesus said, "Whosoever...shall have whatsoever he saith." We can draw five simple conclusions from this scripture:

> 1. If it were God's will for the mountain to be there, Jesus would not have told you to move it.
> 2. If you only knew what was on the other side of your mountain, you would move it.
> 3. If it is there, you can move it. There is no mountain in the sphere of your life that you cannot move.
> 4. Your mountain needs to hear your voice.
> 5. If what you have in life is all up to God, Jesus never would have said Mark 11:23.

If there is a mountain in your way, "Quark it!" It will obey you. God is holding you responsible to "frame your world" with His Word. The devil would like to frame your world with doubt, fear, depression, sickness, and poverty, but the Word of God will put him on the run.

Jesus told you to speak to the mountain. The mountain has been speaking to you, telling you how big it is, how long it has been there, and that it is impossible to move. Some people have actually gotten into denial about the mountain or the obstacles in their lives. They say, "There is no mountain, there is no mountain." But they are just hiding their eyes and pretending their mountain is not there. Don't get into denial. Someone said, "De Nile is a river in Egypt." Jesus said for you to speak to the mountain, not deny its existence. Don't talk to God about it. Talk to the mountain. Dial up the mountain. Dial 1-800-MOUNTAIN. For most people, it is a local call! Talk to your mountain directly and tell it to be removed and cast into the sea. It will be as though it had never been there! "Quark it!"

OUR IDENTIFICATION

WITH CHRIST

DEMANDS THE IDENTICAL

CONFESSION OF FAITH.

GALATIANS 2:20

6

THE LANGUAGE OF
REDEMPTION
CHAPTER SIX

The dictionary defines "language" as:

- The expression or communication of thoughts and feelings by means of vocal sounds.
- The particular form or manner of selecting and combining words characteristic of a person, group, etc.; form, style, or kind of expression in words; as the language of poetry.
- The particular words and phrases of a profession, group, etc., as, the language of the army.

The most important language in the world is the language of redemption. We must learn to understand and speak the language of the Gospel of Christ. As with any language, you must always hear it before you can speak it. Since I was 17 years old, I have preached frequently in East Africa. I loved the sound of Swahili and endeavored to learn as much of it as possible when I was there.

When I first went there in 1970, many in Tanzania, now Kenya, knew English. It was known as "the money language." If you knew English, you were more valuable in the job market and made more money than other people. All the younger students were encouraged to learn English. It also increased your international ability.

I thought "the money language" was an interesting phrase. The Gospel of Christ is the salvation language, the healing language, the victory language, and the blessing language.

The language of redemption is what happened in the death, burial, and resurrection of Christ and what He is doing for us right now, interceding for us at the right hand of the Father. We must learn what happened when Jesus took His blood into Heaven and purchased our eternal redemption.

THE WORD OF FAITH

We must learn to speak the language of redemption that the Apostle Paul called "the word of faith" (Romans 10:8). The Gospel in English, French, Swahili, Spanish, Japanese, and other languages is the power of God. The vocabulary of salvation and the tenses make a sound that releases the power of God. The phrase "Christ hath redeemed us" is in the past tense, which means it has already been taken care of at the cross. He hath blessed us. He hath healed us. He hath delivered us. He hath translated us. These are all past tense. Since He hath, by faith we have. Now faith is. In Christ, we must learn a new language — the language of God. We must speak the word of faith, "the money language" of heaven. Faith is heaven's currency.

SPEAK TO THE ROCK

You will remember that in the Old Testament when Moses struck the rock, water gushed out to supply the whole nation of Israel as they went through the wilderness. The next time they needed water, God told Moses to speak to the rock. But Moses was angry, and he smote the rock instead. God became angry with Moses and later refused to allow him to enter the Promised Land (Exodus 17:6, Numbers 20:8-12, 1 Corinthians 10:4).

Not only did Moses disobey God when he smote the rock, he destroyed the parallel between the Rock which is Christ and the picture of our redemption. The Rock Jesus was smitten once on the cross.

The book of Hebrews says over and over again, "once" Jesus purchased our redemption. What Jesus did once was done so well it will never have to be done again (Hebrews 9:12).

Two thousand years ago, Jesus, the Rock, was smitten. Now when you speak to the Rock, the water will freely flow. As you speak the Word of God, there is full provision for your every need. So speak to the Rock. The Promised Land is yours today!

THE GIFT OF GAB

Scientists and anthropologists are still attempting to understand creation and what man is. What makes man different from the rest of creation? We know from Genesis that man was made in the image of God. We know that man is a spirit being, he has a soul, and he lives in a body (1 Thessalonians 5:23).

I recently found this interesting article, "The Gift of Gab," by Matt Cartmill in ***Discover*** magazine. Here are some excerpts:

> *People can talk. Other animals can't. They can all communicate in one way or another but their whinnies and wiggles don't do the job that language does. The birds and beasts can use their signals to attract, threaten, or alert each other, but they can't ask questions, strike bargains, tell stories, or lay out a plan of action. Those skills make Homosapiens a uniquely successful, powerful, and dangerous mammal. Other creatures' signals carry only a few limited kinds of information about what's happening at the moment, but language lets us tell each other in limitless detail about what used to be or will be or might be...Without language, we would be only a sort of upright chimpanzee with funny feet and clever hands. With it, we are the self-possessed masters of the planet.*

THE POWER TO CHOOSE

You can see that language is unique to man. God created us eternal spirit beings in His image with the power of speech. James 3 is clear that the tongue determines our direction and destiny. We have the power to choose blessing or cursing, life or death (Deuteronomy 30:19). Words determine the boundaries and set the limits on our lives.

> *"By thy words thou shalt be justified, and by thy words thou shalt be condemned." - Matthew 12:37*

The Gospel is the language of faith. Believing and speaking are the two most fundamental ingredients in faith. I have heard the testimonies of two people who died and came back from the dead. One was from Zaire, and the other was from the United States. I thought it was interesting they both said when their spirits returned to their bodies, they entered through their mouths. God breathed the breath of life into Adam's mouth. If your spirit enters or exits your body through your mouth, why would the impact of words or speech on our lives seem strange?

> *"Death and life are in the power of the tongue..."*
> *- Proverbs 18:21*

NEVER RUN AT YOUR GIANT

WITH YOUR MOUTH SHUT!

1 SAMUEL 17

7

WINNING THE WAR
OF WORDS
CHAPTER SEVEN

"Never run at your giant with your mouth shut!" These are the words the Lord spoke to me as a key to killing my giants. We all face many giants in life that must be conquered before we can receive and do all that God has for us. As you know, some of these giants can be persistent. Speaking the Word of God releases God's power to win in each conflict.

Winning the war of words is necessary to win the fight of faith. 1 Samuel 17 gives us a picture of the faith-filled words that were spoken and determined the outcome of the war. As you can see from the following passage, David's word-war did not begin with Goliath; it actually began with Saul. You could call this the pre-fight warm up. Some people lose before they ever get to the real fight. Let's see how David won:

> *"And David said to Saul, Let no man's heart fail because of him; thy servant will go and fight with this Philistine. And Saul said to David, Thou art not able to go against this Philistine to fight with him: for thou art but a youth, and he a man of war from his youth. And David said unto Saul, Thy servant kept his father's sheep, and there came a lion, and a bear, and took a lamb out of the flock: And I went out after him, and smote him, and delivered it out of his mouth: and when he arose against me, I caught him by his beard, and smote him and slew him. Thy servant slew both the lion and the bear: and this uncircumcised Philistine shall be as one of them, seeing he hath defied the armies of the living God. David said moreover, The Lord that delivered me out of the paw of the lion, and out of the paw of the bear, he will deliver me out of the hand of this Philistine. And Saul said unto David, Go, and the Lord be with thee. And when the Philistine looked about, and saw David, he disdained him: for he was but a youth, and ruddy,*

and of a fair countenance. And the Philistine said unto David, Am I a dog, that thou comest to me with staves? And the Philistine cursed David by his gods. And the Philistine said to David, Come to me, and I will give thy flesh unto the fowls of the air, and to the beasts of the field. Then said David to the Philistine, Thou comest to me with a sword, and with a spear, and with a shield: but I come to thee in the name of the Lord of hosts, the God of the armies of Israel, whom thou hast defied. This day will the Lord deliver thee into mine hand; and I will smite thee, and take thine head from thee; and I will give the carcases of the host of the Philistines this day unto the fowls of the air, and to the wild beasts of the earth; that all the earth may know that there is a God in Israel. And all this assembly shall know that the Lord saveth not with sword and spear: for the battle is the Lord's, and he will give you into our hands. And it came to pass, when the Philistine arose, and came and drew nigh to meet David, that David hasted, and ran toward the army to meet the Philistine. And David put his hand in his bag, and took thence a stone, and slang it, and smote the Philistine in his forehead, that the stone sunk into his forehead; and he fell upon his face to the earth.

So David prevailed over the Philistine with a sling and with a stone, and smote the Philistine, and slew him; but there was no sword in the hand of David. Therefore David ran, and stood upon the Philistine, and took his sword, and drew it out of the sheath thereof, and slew him, and cut off his head therewith. And when the Philistines saw their champion was dead, they fled."

- 1 Samuel 17: 32-37, 42-51

This is the classic story of David and Goliath. The real battle was won before David actually killed Goliath. A war of words had to be won before victory could be consummated. Never run at your giant with your mouth shut!

Before David ran at Goliath a war of words went on. Goliath said - David said - Goliath said - David said - David ran toward the Philistine - David prevailed over the Philistine. You know the story well. We all love it. I want to emphasize that David won the war of words before he won the victory. Never let the devil have the last word.

Another example of winning the war of words is found in Matthew 4. Jesus won the war of words with Satan and refused to give in to temptation.

"And when the tempter came to him [Jesus], he said, If thou be the Son of God, command that these stones be made bread. But he answered and said, It is written, Man shall not live by bread alone, but by every word that proceedeth out of the mouth of God. Then the devil taketh him up into the holy city, and setteth him on a pinnacle of the temple, And saith unto him, If thou be the Son of God, cast thyself down: for it is written, He shall give his angels charge concerning thee: and in their hands they shall bear thee up lest at any time thou dash thy foot against a stone. Jesus said unto him, It is written again, Thou shalt not tempt the Lord thy God. Again, the devil taketh him up into an exceeding high mountain, and showeth him all the kingdoms of the world, and the glory of them; And saith unto him, All these things will I give thee, if thou wilt fall down and worship me. And saith Jesus unto him, Get thee hence, Satan: for it is written, Thou shalt worship the Lord thy God, and him only shalt thou serve. Then the devil leaveth him, and, behold angels came and ministered unto him." - Matthew 4:3-11

In the same way, we see Jesus face Satan in the wilderness in Matthew 4. Jesus defeated Satan by speaking the Word of God. Satan said - Jesus said - Satan said - Jesus said - Satan said - Jesus said. Notice that the Lord Jesus Christ won the war of words and put the devil on the run. Even Jesus had to "say" three times before the devil left. The power of speaking the Word of God is evident and necessary to win the fight of faith.

The spirit of faith believes and speaks (2 Corinthians 4:13). Jesus said in Mark 11:23, "Whosoever shall say ... believe that those things which he saith ...he shall have whatsoever he saith." In that verse Jesus clearly tells us how faith works. He said, "believe" once but He said, "say, saith, saith" three times. Faith is released by speaking. If you are silent, you lose by default. You must win the war of words to win in every conflict.

PRISONERS OF WORDS

A war of words is going on in each of our lives every day. Winning that war will determine life or death, blessing or cursing. Many people are held hostage by their words; they are prisoners of words. Proverbs 6:2 says, "Thou art snared with the words of thy mouth, thou art taken with the words of thy mouth." The Jerusalem Bible says, "...

through words of yours you have been entrapped." Basic English says, "...the sayings of your lips have overcome you." According to Proverbs 18:21, "Death and life are in the power of the tongue." James 3 tells us that the direction and destiny of our life is determined by the tongue.

We must win the war of words before we win in any area of life. God has supplied the ammunition, the Word, to win in every area. There is life, healing, joy, victory, and blessing in the Word of God. You are a believer and you must speak what you believe for victory to be yours.

The confession of your lips that has grown out of faith in your heart will absolutely defeat the adversary in every combat. That means Satan cannot win if you will hold fast to your confession and allow your words to register on your spirit.

GOD'S WORD IN YOUR MOUTH

You can see why the devil would fight against you getting the Word in your mouth. Everything Jesus did is activated by getting the Word in your mouth and in your heart. Reinhard Bonnke said the Lord told him, "My Word in your mouth is just as powerful as My Word in My mouth."

The thing you need to focus on is getting the Word in your mouth. When you get the Word in your mouth, you have the answer. The answer is already in the Word!

You are not in any way trying to replace God. Instead, you are releasing God. You have that authority as a believer. There is so much power in this that you can see why the devil would want to gain control of your mouth.

You have the same spirit of faith that David had, Paul had, and the Lord Jesus had. Fight the good fight of faith by believing and speaking. Say what God has done for you in the plan of redemption. Say what Jesus has done through His blood and the power of His resurrection. God's Word spoken through your lips wins in every conflict!

IF YOU ARE SILENT

YOU LOSE BY DEFAULT.

FAITH WORKS BY SPEAKING.

MARK 11:23

8

CONFESS UP
CHAPTER EIGHT

"...Attentively consider the Apostle and High Priest of our confession – Jesus."
- Hebrews 3:1; Rotherham

"...Inasmuch then as we have a great High Priest Who has [already] ascended and passed through the heavens, Jesus the Son of God, let us hold fast our confession [of faith in Him]."
- Hebrews 4:14; Amplified

Using the word "confession" in our society conjures up the thought of someone admitting to something negative. When a person is trying to get someone else to confess or admit to something negative, they will use the expression own up or admit it. Sometimes a shorter version is used, "fess up."

1 John 1:9 speaks of confessing to the Lord our sin in order to restore fellowship with Him. However, the New Testament has much more to say about confession in a positive light than in a negative light.

Many believers today need to recognize the power of positive confession. In other words, they need to own up to the reality of all that Jesus has done and is doing for them. They need to "own up" to the reality of redemption and who they are in Christ.

You need to spend time every day owning up to who Jesus is and who you are in Him. We should all fess up to the power of the blood of Jesus and that in Him we are redeemed, forgiven, healed, and blessed. It is necessary for us to own up to our redemption.

CONFESSION PRECEDES POSSESSION

Nothing will establish you and build your faith as quickly as the confession of who you are and what you have in Christ — your redemption.

Confession precedes possession. Confession is the beginning of possession. Confession is owning up. We can own up or down. Confess up! Jesus is the Apostle and High Priest of our confession. He represents and responds to our words. He needs us to hold fast to our confession of faith in Him He is waiting for us to say something that agrees with all He has done. He literally needs us to say something of faith that activates His work and power.

Your identification with Christ is activated by the identical confession of your mouth that "I am who God says I am. I have what God says I have. I can do what God says I can do." We must say the same thing that God says about us in Christ. If you are not impressed with who you are in Christ, you simply have not seen Him lately. He is glorified and all-powerful, and you are in Him. You must own up to it! Fess up!

The Greek word translated profession or confession in the New Testament means "to say the same thing." The power of positive confession means to say the same thing that the Word of God says about your situation. This is such a powerful truth because it is the way we are saved.

> *"For with the heart man believeth unto righteousness; and with the mouth confession is made unto salvation." - Romans 10:10*

We are saved when we believe in our heart and confess with our mouth that Jesus is Lord. Confession is owning up to the lordship of Jesus and owning up to all that salvation includes. When powerful words are spoken from a believer's mouth the human spirit is recreated and eternal life is imparted to a person.

I like what F. F. Bosworth said, "A spiritual law that few recognize is that our confession rules us. It is what we confess with our lips that really dominates our inner being. Nothing will establish you and build your faith as quickly as confession. The confession of your lips that has grown out of faith in your heart will absolutely defeat the adversary in every combat. God can be no bigger in you than you confess Him to be."

Sometimes people trying to be humble are just being ignorant. Yes, we should humble ourselves under the mighty hand of God that He may exalt us in due time. However, there are things that are timely and things that are timeless. There are things that require the right season, and there are things concerning your redemption that are open season all year. God is always ready to save, heal, deliver, and bless. Jesus has already passed through the heavens; He is now watching over and waiting for your confession. It is now open season and all things are possible!

OWN UP! ADMIT IT!

"Fight the good fight of faith, lay hold on eternal life, whereunto thou art also called, and hast professed a good profession before many witnesses."
- *1 Timothy 6:12*

The Holy Spirit said through the Apostle Paul that the good fight of faith requires a good confession. The fight of faith is not a losing fight; it is a winning fight. The winning fight requires a winning confession. Jesus has fought the battle for us and won. Our identification with Him demands the identical confession of faith. We win by saying the same thing.

The spirit of faith declares the outcome in the middle of adversity. We hold fast to our confession. We can see the end from the beginning of trouble. We consider Jesus and fix our eyes and our confession on Him.

Own up to your victory in Christ Jesus by saying, "Thanks be unto God who always causeth us to triumph in Christ," 2 Corinthians 2:14.

Settle for nothing less than 100 percent victory. Victory is yours now. Confess up! Own up! Fess up! Admit it! You are a new creature in Christ. You are the righteousness of God in Him. Say now, "In Christ, I am blessed."

> *"That the communication of thy faith may become*
> *effectual by the acknowledging of every good thing*
> *which is in you in Christ Jesus." -Philemon 6*

> *"...full recognition and appreciation and*
> *understanding and precise knowledge of e very good*
> *thing that is ours in (our identification with)*
> *Christ Jesus." –Amplified*

For our faith to become fully effective, we must continually acknowledge every good thing that is in us in Christ. Sometimes our faith is like an automobile engine that has eight cylinders, but is only working on five or six. Much more power is available when we are working on all eight cylinders. Sometimes we are putting along — choking — because we are not acknowledging every good thing in us in Christ.

There is a wealth of good things in you in Christ. They are not just in Christ, they are in you because you are in Christ. More than 130 scriptures in the New Testament use the phrases, In Christ, In Him, and In Whom. Every time you see those two words, underline them and say, "That's who I am, and that's what I have." A good place to start is 2 Corinthians 5:17, 2 Corinthians 5:21, and 1 Corinthians 1:30.

FITTED TO YOUR LIPS

"For it is a pleasant thing if thou keep them within thee; they shall withal be fitted in thy lips. That thy trust may be in the Lord…" -Proverbs 22:18, 19

The Word of God is custom fitted for your lips. The Word of God was made to be spoken. Confession is fundamental to faith. E.W. Kenyon said, "Confession builds the road over which faith carries its mighty cargo." The Amplified Bible translates Proverbs 22:18 this way, "For it will be pleasant if you keep them in your mind [believing them]; your lips will be accustomed to [confessing] them." I like that. Your lips should be accustomed to confessing the Word of God. The Word is custom fitted or tailor made for your mouth and your situation.

The Word of God was spoken before it was written and it was written so it could be spoken. Jesus is the Apostle and High Priest of your confession. "Whosoever shall say …he shall have whatsoever he saith …" (Mark 11:23).

Jesus is literally waiting for you to confess. As we saw, the word "confess" literally means "to say the same thing." In other words, He has already said something about you, but He needs you to say the same thing. Will you say the same thing?

Every benefit and blessing that is in us in Christ must be acknowledged and declared. For salvation to work for you, it must be in your mouth. For prosperity to work for you, it must be in your mouth. Say, "I am blessed coming in and going out. I am the head and not the tail, above and not beneath," Deuteronomy 28. For healing to work for you, it must be in your mouth. Say, "...by his stripes I was healed," 1 Peter 2:24. The Word will heal you if you will continually confess it – own up to it. There is healing and prosperity in the Word. So say what God says about you.

AN EXPLOSION OF POWER

"And they overcame him [Satan] by the blood of the Lamb, and by the word of their testimony..."
-Revelation 12:11

The tremendous power in the blood of Jesus is activated by adding your testimony to it. Your confession, testimony, and declaration of the blood of Jesus put the devil on the run. Satan, the accuser of the brethren, is constantly accusing us. The blood of Jesus when mixed with faith always overcomes the enemy. Romans 3:25 says, "...through faith in His blood."

Mixing faith with the blood of Jesus is like mixing

nitro with glycerin. There is always an explosion of power. Our lips should be accustomed to confessing the power of the blood of Jesus and all that has been purchased for us in Him.

Make a personal daily list of scriptures that acknowledge who you are, what you have, and what you can do because you are in Christ. Own up to what God has made you in Christ. God is always right, and confession is agreeing with God and His Word. Every time you speak the Word, you are agreeing with God.

Say it now: "Christ hath redeemed me from the curse of the law. I am redeemed," Galatians 3:13.

Say it to yourself quietly when you can. Talk to yourself. Say it out loud when it's appropriate. Then repeat it over and over again. There is a fight to faith but it's a good fight because it's one you win.

Next, say it until your whole being swings into harmony and into line with the Word of God. In other words, say it until your spirit starts lining up with the words you speak. They register on your heart and on your mind. You start seeing yourself healed and blessed.

As you hold fast to your confession of faith, you will find that your faith will advance and be more effective. Confess up! Never run at your giant with your mouth shut.

YOUR MOUNTAIN

NEEDS TO HEAR

YOUR VOICE!

MARK 11:23

9

THE SOUND OF FAITH
CHAPTER NINE

Several years ago, I went hunting for coyote in Arizona with a friend who was an avid hunter. We got up early in the morning, while it was still dark, and put on camouflage outfits — pants, shirt, hat, and boots. My shotgun and pistol were camouflaged. Even my hands and face were covered with camouflage paint. My friend also gave me a pair of camouflage glasses with a camouflage veil. I was so camouflaged, when I looked in the mirror, I couldn't even see myself!

We went out on a mountainside and sat on the ground under a big bush, with camouflage netting wrapped around us. My friend began to call the coyotes with a little wooden call he blew. It made a loud, squealing noise like the sound of a wounded rabbit. When the coyotes heard the squeal of the hurt rabbit they would come for what they thought was a nice meal.

My friend and I stayed under the bush for several hours, calling the coyotes. I was starting to feel pretty ridiculous, because we were two grown men dressed like Rambo sitting there making crazy noises.

We never got a coyote that day, but I learned a valuable lesson. The Lord began to talk to me about faith. Many people, even Spirit-filled Christians, are continually whining and speaking defeat and depression, calling up the "coyote" of failure. Their "wounded rabbit" call attracts the devil, and he comes to devour them for lunch! It is open season on the person who whines, complains, and constantly speaks fear and failure.

That kind of attitude opens the door to the devil. We have many "wounded rabbits" in the church who need to change their sound. I don't believe the devil can kill anyone anytime he wants. He must get you to agree with doubt and fear before he can harm you.

AGREE WITH GOD

Faith agrees with God and shuts the door on the devil. By changing your sound to a bold declaration of who you are in Christ Jesus, you will begin to attract the blessings of

God in a greater measure.

How does one change a lifelong habit of "wounded rabbit" language? A good place to begin is Philemon 6, "That the communication of thy faith may become effectual by the acknowledging of every good thing which is in you in Christ Jesus."

The Apostle Paul is saying that our faith will become effective by acknowledging every good thing that is in us because we are in Christ. Many good things are in us who are in Christ. We need to acknowledge our identification with Christ by boldly saying, "...The Lord is my helper, and I will not fear... (Hebrews 13:6)." I am who God says I am. I have what God says I have. I can do what God says I can do.

We will no longer speak the cry of defeat, fear, and doubt — but by acknowledging our identification with Christ, we will begin making the sounds of victory, health, prosperity, and blessings.

THE SPIRIT OF FAITH

WILL MAKE YOU SWING OUT

OVER HELL ON A CORNSTALK

AND SPIT IN THE DEVIL'S EYE.

10

THE SPIRIT OF FAITH

CHAPTER TEN

"We having the same spirit of faith, according as it is written, I believed and therefore have I spoken; we also believe and therefore speak."

- 2 Corinthians 4:13

As I meditated on this verse, I got these words, "The principles of faith are taught, but the spirit of faith is caught." Jesus spent much of His time teaching. The teaching ministry of Jesus was valuable and necessary. If people automatically knew how to receive from God and walk with Him, why did Jesus spend so much time teaching? The fact is, we must have the teaching of the Word of God.

Jesus' teachings were so plain and simple, anyone could understand exactly what He meant. He said what He meant, and He meant what He said. His illustrations are so clear, you would need a theologian to misunderstand them.

CATCH THE SPIRIT OF FAITH AND PASS IT ON

The great thing about Jesus is that He will stay with you until you understand it. However, there is more to faith than principles. Remember Paul said, "We having the same spirit of faith..." 2 Corinthians 4:13. You must catch the spirit of faith. The spirit of faith must be imparted. You can catch it by associating with people who have it. The spirit of faith is contagious! When you have it, you pass it on to others.

Abraham passed it on to his children and grandchildren. Joshua caught it from Moses. Elisha caught it from Elijah and doubled it. David's mighty men in the cave of Adullam were not so mighty until they caught the spirit of faith from David. The disciples caught it from Jesus. Timothy caught it from Paul. These are just a few examples in the Word of God. Many are still catching the spirit of faith today. Even if you already have it, you can have more and double it, as Elisha did.

FAITH HAS NO LIMITS

The spirit of faith is unlimited. Jesus said in Mark 9:23, "If thou canst believe, all things are possible to him that believeth." The spirit of faith takes the limits off God. God is not only a big, big, big God; but He is also a good, good, good God! Take the limits off of His ability and His goodness. God can do and wants to do things for you that are so glorious, there will be no doubt that He did it. I have found that God is so good, He will do things for you that you wouldn't do for yourself.

The spirit of faith believes and speaks the unlimited possibilities of God. "For with God nothing shall be impossible," Luke 1:37. The spirit of faith will make a tadpole slap a whale. It will make you swing out over hell on a cornstalk and spit in the devil's eye. You can never achieve the impossible if you never attempt the impossible. The spirit of faith will position you to possess God's best blessings.

YOU ARE ONE STEP AWAY FROM A MIRACLE

Some time ago, I was watching a nationally televised NCAA football game. The team was ranked in the top ten in the country, and the quarterback was one of the best in college football. The play had been called in the huddle, and the players were lined up at the line of scrimmage to run the play. The quarterback came up to the line, began to yell out the numbers, and bent over to receive the snap of the ball when he realized that he was behind the guard instead of the center.

If you know anything about American football, you know the center is the one who snaps the ball to the quarterback, not the guard. In the middle of his calling the play, he took one step over right behind the center and hollered, "Hut, hut, hut." The ball was hiked to him, and the play was run successfully.

I laughed a little while I was watching this. Then the Lord spoke to me, using that illustration. He said, "Some people need to make a small adjustment if they are going to receive from Me. Some people are only one step away from a miracle!" It isn't far from the guard to the center. Some people look like they are lined up with the Word of God, and they sound like they are ready to run the play, but really there is a small adjustment that must be made before things work right. It isn't difficult, but it requires humbling yourself and moving into a closer agreement with God's ways, power, and plan. Sometimes, it is just one small step over to receive from God.

BELIEVE IT AND SAY IT

The spirit of faith works by believing and speaking. The spirit of faith requires your "speaker" to be hooked up to your "believer." In other words, for faith to work properly, it must be in your heart and in your mouth (Romans 10:8-10; Mark 11:23).

The word spoken to you must be spoken through you. The spirit of faith does not guarantee that you won't have any storms in life. The storms of life come to everyone. However, the spirit of faith is what enables you to face the storms and overcome. The Apostle Paul illustrated this while at sea in the middle of a life-threatening storm.

> *"Wherefore, sirs, be of good cheer: for I believe God, that it shall be even as it was told me."*
> *- Acts 27:25*

The spirit of faith will put you over. In the middle of trouble, Paul said, "Cheer up, everyone! I believe God."

One person with the spirit of faith can change the destinies of many others. Paul said, "It shall be even as it was told me." God's Word is the foundation for our faith. The spirit of faith believes and speaks. What does the Word say? What has God spoken to you? Believe it and say it. It will put you over. It will take you through the storms of life and enable you to finish your course.

WHEN FAITH COMETH, YOU KNOWETH

"So then faith cometh by hearing, and hearing by the word of God," Romans 10:17. When faith cometh, you knoweth (that's not good English, but you get the message)! It is no great secret where faith comes from. Faith is the by-product of the Word of God. Notice it says by "hearing and hearing" the Word of God. Sometimes we don't understand it the first time around, so God will repeat it.

Has God ever told you anything more than once? He has told me some things many times. Sometimes He will say the same thing exactly, and sometimes He will use someone to say it a little differently so I can understand it. The Word of God is faith food.

WHEN FAITH COMETH, FEAR GOETH

When faith cometh, fear goeth! Fear leaveth when faith cometh. God is a faith God (Hebrews 11:6). God works by faith. The devil is a fear devil. The devil works by fear. There are 365 times in the Bible where we are told "fear not." Jesus said, "Fear not: believe only," Luke 8:50.

> *"We having the same spirit of faith, according as it is written, I believed, and therefore have I spoken; we also believe, and therefore speak."*
> *- 2 Corinthians 4:13*

The Apostle Paul quotes the psalmist David, "I believed, therefore have I spoken...," Psalm 116:10. There can be no doubt that David had a spirit of faith. He killed a lion, a bear, the giant Goliath, and more than 10,000 Philistines. Case closed — the man had a spirit of faith.

However, in Psalms, we see David dealing with an overcoming fear. In Psalm 27:1, David declared, "The Lord is my light and my salvation; whom shall I fear? The Lord is the strength of my life; of whom shall I be afraid?" Here we see David believing and speaking. The spirit of faith requires both.

FAITH DETERMINES YOUR DESTINY

In the midst of adversity, David was overcoming fear. The spirit of faith is necessary to do the will of God. Hebrews 11:6 says, "Without faith it is impossible to please him: for he that cometh to God must believe that he is, and that he is a rewarder of them that diligently seek him." Faith is absolutely necessary to please God and do the will of God.

Dr. Lilian B. Yeomans said, "God has tied Himself irrevocably to human cooperation in the execution of divine purposes. He has made man's faith a determining factor in the work of redemption."

Although God is sovereign, He has tied Himself to human cooperation to work out His divine purposes. Jesus said, "...according to your faith be it unto you," Matthew 9:29. As you know, the first ingredient in the spirit of faith is to believe. In Mark 5, when the woman with the issue of blood touched Jesus, she got healed. Jesus said, "Daughter, your faith has made you whole." Brother Kenneth E. Hagin (Dad Hagin) said the Lord told him, "If her faith made her whole, then your faith will make you whole."

FEAR NOT, ONLY BELIEVE

At the time the woman was healed, Jesus was on the way to the house of Jairus, the ruler of the synagogue, to pray for his daughter, who was dying. When Jesus told the woman, "Your faith has made you whole," Jairus' servants came from his house, saying, "Don't trouble Jesus any longer. Your daughter is already dead." When Jesus heard them say that to Jairus, He gave him some vital information, "Fear not, only believe."

There is a fight to faith. At that moment, Jairus could have believed the bad report, gotten in fear, and given up on his miracle. But Jesus said, "Let Me tell you what to do in this situation, fear not, only believe."

When the doctors told us that my wife, Trina, had a brain tumor, all the specialists and neurosurgeons gave their opinions and bad reports for seven days. Friends called and asked, "What are you going to do?" All I said was, "I don't know what I'm going to do, but I know what I'm not going to do." I decided to resist the spirit of fear and "fear not." That means I remained in faith and continued to believe God. I believed the Word of God. I choose to fear not, only believe. Believing is a choice.

Fear has several relatives and companions: doubt, anxiety, stress, and worry. These all stem from the same fear. It is impossible to have a spirit of faith and a spirit of fear at the same time. When you have a spirit of faith, you don't have a spirit of fear.

The Bible says that in the last days, people's hearts will fail them because of fear (Luke 21:26). In 2 Timothy 1:7, Paul writes, "For God hath not given us a spirit of fear; but of power, and of love, and of a sound mind." If God didn't give you a spirit of fear, where did you get it?

Fear comes from the devil. The devil is a fear devil. God is a faith God. Jesus said in Mark 9:23, "...If thou canst believe, all things are possible to him that believeth." This means, "Fear not, only believe."

YOU CHOOSE FAITH OR FEAR

Not only do you believe, but you also have to say what you believe. There will be a fight in the worst of your circumstances. There will be a moment when you must choose to either be full of fear or believe God. Jesus grabbed Jairus right in the middle of his choice and gave him a word. Jesus will give you a word right in the middle of your crisis, too. He knows what others are telling you; He knows the doubts that are flooding your mind and the way the devil is attacking you. Jesus hears and says, "I'd like to interrupt the fear and doubt and give you a word from heaven; fear not only believe."

Jairus might have told Jesus, "I don't know what is going on. I don't know how all this happened; but if you told me to fear not and believe only, that is where my responsibility ends. That is all I have to do, and I'll let You take care of the rest." You don't have to change the whole situation. You only have to do your part, and your part is to fear not, only believe. Jesus said, "If you can stay in faith, I'll come to your house. I'll bring my faith friends — Peter, James, and John."

Jairus' relatives and friends were already planning his daughter's funeral when Jesus told them, "Get out! It's not over. She's not dead; she's just sleeping." When the devil says it is all over, Jesus says it is not all over; it has just been delayed for a little while. Would you like Jesus to visit your house, bring some of His disciples, and throw out doubt, fear, confusion, stress, and anxiety — and breathe new life into dead things? Jesus said to fear not, only believe. When you have a spirit of faith, you say what you believe.

God can take care of you. He can work in your life and undo everything the devil has done. God has power. He has angels on assignment to watch over you. He is able to raise the dead, heal the sick, cast out devils, and turn your whole life around. When He speaks, faith comes, and when faith comes fear goes!

DEAL WITH FEAR SUPERNATURALLY

There is a fight to faith. You cannot deal with fear naturally. You cannot reason with fear. Fear is a spirit; a supernatural problem. You have to have a word from God — the word of faith.

> *"So then faith cometh by hearing, and hearing by the word of God." - Romans 10:17*

When faith comes, healing comes, blessing comes, joy comes, and fear goes. When faith comes, you know. Faith is the substance of things hoped for, the evidence of things not seen. When faith comes, the substance comes, and you know you have it.

The devil would like to starve your faith. Smith Wigglesworth said, "Some people feed their bodies three hot meals a day, and their spirits one cold snack a week, and wonder why they're weak in faith." You must feed on the Word of God to be strong in faith. Hear it, meditate on it, speak it, and go over and over it until you feel the substance of faith rise up in your spirit. Faith cometh!

CLOSE THE DOOR ON THE DEVIL

There are more than 100 different kinds of fear. These fears can be irrational, but since fear is of the devil, it does not have to be rational. Here is a list of some of the phobias that plague mankind:

Acrophobia: fear of heights

Claustrophobia: fear of enclosed places

Agoraphobia: fear of outdoors and open spaces (affects 2 million Americans)

Anthropophobia: fear of people

Cynophobia: fear of dogs

Kleptophobia: fear of thieves

Aquaphobia: fear of water

Brontophobia: fear of thunderstorms

Dentophobia: fear of dentists

Skiaphobia: fear of shadows

Cardiophobia: fear of heart disease

Triskaidekaphobia: fear of the number 13

Arachibutyrophobia: fear of getting peanut butter stuck to the roof of the mouth

Amaxophobia: fear of riding in vehicles

Anuptaphobia: fear of staying single

Hematophobia: fear of the sight of blood

Peniaphobia: fear of poverty

Tropophobia: fear of changes

Gephyrophobia: fear of crossing bridges

Pantaphobia: the morbid dread of everything

There are too many phobias to list. Psychologists say that Thanatophobia, the fear of death, is the root of all fears. If you have a spirit of fear, you did not get it from God.

Fear opens the door to the devil and fear is connected to the lack of power, lack of love, and mental problems. The spirit of fear must be dealt with supernaturally.

The Word of God breaks the spirit of fear. Faith comes by hearing, and hearing by the Word of God. When faith comes, fear goes. There is faith, power, love, and mental soundness in the Word of God.

Hebrews 2:14,15 says that Jesus, through death, destroyed the power of the devil and delivered those, who through fear of death, were subject to its bondage during all their lifetime. Jesus has delivered us from the power and the control of the devil!

David wrote, "I sought the Lord, and he heard me, and delivered me from all my fears," Psalm 34:4. David had a spirit of faith, but he still had to overcome the enemy of fear. Fear not only opens the door to the devil, it will also paralyze you from moving with God's plan for your life.

THE VOICE OF FAITH

You can be free from all your fears. When faith comes, fear goes. Do not cast away your confidence. Faith in God is faith in His Word. Believe God, believe the Word, and speak with the voice of faith. Your faith is voice-activated.

Sometimes you must get radical when you deal with fear, doubt, and anxiety. Fear is a spirit, and it will come against your mind. You must deal with it by saying, "You foul spirit of fear, I resist you in the name of Jesus. I refuse to doubt. I fear not; I only believe. I made that choice. Now get out!"

When the supernatural comes into contact with the natural, something has to give! When the power of God is in manifestation, it will hit you on the top of your head, go down your back, and get in your legs. You will say, "It's all over me, and it's keeping me alive. I shall not die, but I shall live and declare the works of God."

We know that with faith you always get it on the inside before you get it on the outside. There is a fight of faith necessary to lay hold of the blessings of God. Get a grip on the spirit of faith — catch it and keep it!

WINNING THE WAR OF WORDS

IS NECESSARY TO WIN

THE FIGHT OF FAITH

1 TIMOTHY 6:12

11

THE FIGHT OF FAITH
CHAPTER ELEVEN

One of Abraham Lincoln's favorite stories was about one of his neighbors who had a little dog that could whip all the big dogs. When someone asked the man how his little dog could whip all the big dogs, he said, "Your big dog is not really ready to fight until the fight is half over. My little dog stays mad!"

Don't wait any longer before you really use your faith to lay hold of what belongs to you. Right now, set goals of prayer, faith, and blessing for your life and "stay mad." Keep your faith focused all the time. Refuse to give one inch to the devil, defeat, or discouragement.

> *"Fight the good fight of faith, lay hold on eternal life, whereunto thou art also called and hast professed a good profession before many witnesses."*
> - 1 Timothy 6:12

Are you ready to fight? The faith fight is the only fight believers are called to fight. We are not called to fight other people. We really are not called to fight the devil, because he is a defeated foe. Jesus defeated him 2,000 years ago.

One of Satan's strategies is to entice the believer out of the arena of faith and into the arena of feelings, sight, or circumstances. You must stay in the arena of faith, because that is where the victory is won. Another strategy of the devil is discouragement.

During the Korean War, a company of American soldiers took a particular hill in Korea 13 times and lost it every time. However, on the fourteenth attempt, they took the hill and kept it. You may experience setbacks and delays in your life, but your faith fight is a good fight, because you win!

NEVER RUN AT YOUR GIANT WITH YOUR MOUTH SHUT

Don't let the devil shut your mouth. When the devil talks trash to you, talk it right back to him. He'll try to intimidate you, just like Goliath talked to David. Do you know what David did? He started talking back to Goliath. He said, "I'm going to kill you, cut your head off, hang it in my tent, and feed your body to the birds!"

All of us have giants or things that seem bigger than we are. That's why everyone needs at least one Goliath head hanging in his tent. Some people may think that's stupid, but if you've ever fought a Goliath, you'll want to keep the head in your trophy room, too.

David activated the covenant with his confession and actions. You can do the same thing. Never run at your giant with your mouth shut. Often people run to see what happens, but faith always declares the outcome before the fight ever starts. In other words, the battle is won on the inside before you ever win it on the outside.

Sometimes in the middle of the storm you need to say, "Hold it! I'd like to say a few things before this is over." Anyone can say things after the storm is over. Often people will say afterwards, "I just knew everything was going to turn out all right." Why didn't they say that in the middle of the struggle?

In the middle of the battle you should say, "The victory is mine." The Word spoken to you must be spoken through you. In the midst of the storm at sea, Paul said, "I believe God. It shall be as He said."

Let me tell you who He is. Jesus said, "I am he that liveth, and was dead: and, behold, I am alive for ever more...," Revelation 1:18. I get my words from Him — the One who went through the cross, death, hell, and the grave, and was raised from the dead. I believe God. It shall be as He told me.

THE GOOD FIGHT OF FAITH

If you are in a faith fight now, the devil is going to make sure it's not easy for you. He's going to try to stop it. He will put roadblocks, mountains, difficulties, and hindrances everywhere he can and tell you that God is not faithful and the Word doesn't work. You've got to say, "This is a good fight. It's not a bad fight. I am fighting the good fight of faith. I've got a good confession, and I'm going to enjoy the fight."

There is a fight to faith — a good fight and winning fight. The good faith fight requires a good profession or confession. You must say what you believe to lay hold or possess your victory. Sometimes it is much easier to say how you feel or how things look than to say what you believe.

Paul said in 2 Corinthians 4:13, "We having the same spirit of faith...believe and...speak." Your faith will never rise above your confession. E.W. Kenyon said, "Confession builds the road over which faith hauls its mighty cargo." If your faith is going to get some thing to your house, how would it get there? You will have to build a road or street there.

Your confession of faith should be strong enough for some eighteen-wheelers to carry heaven's cargo to your address. Confession always precedes possession.

If you wonder why only a few things get to your house, perhaps you have built only a narrow path with your words, and you have never taken the time to build an adequate road. If you want to change the road from being a muddy little path with potholes and trees across the way, change your confession!

Sometimes there may be what seems like a delay, but how many years did you spend confessing a footpath? Some years ago, the State of Louisiana completed I-49 from the southern part of the state to the northern part. Even with modern technology and equipment, it took 20 years from start to finish! They started out marking the path, and for years they moved dirt and then finally poured the concrete.

It takes time to build a super-highway. So if you are expecting some major traffic to come to your house, start building the road right now. Remember, confession is the road over which faith carries its mighty cargo.

Although confession builds the road, it will never take the place of prayer. Your confession is born out of rich fellowship with the Father God. I don't mean a superficial relationship, but a heart relationship with the Father, where your spirit is in fellowship with the Lord Jesus. Your confession is born out of that fellowship.

Your words will either complete your faith, or they will defeat your faith. You must boldly confess your redemption in Christ and who you are in Him

WHO YOU ARE IN CHRIST

One of the biggest enemies to faith is a lack of understanding your redemption in Christ. Once you know the truth about redemption, you will enjoy the freedom Jesus purchased for you. Christ has redeemed us, according to Galatians 3:13.

Another enemy to faith is a lack of understanding who you are in Christ. You are well able to possess the land because of your union with Christ. In Him you are redeemed. In Him you are strong. In Him you are blessed. In Him you are forgiven. In Him you are always triumphant!

You must maintain a good confession of who you are in Christ to fight the good fight of faith. You must say, "I am who God says I am. I have what God says I have. I can do what God says I can do."

You can "stay mad" by realizing that Jesus paid too high a price for your freedom for you to remain bound. He paid too high a price for your healing for you to stay sick. He paid too high a price for your prosperity for you to be poor. Jesus purchased your freedom with His own blood (Hebrews 9:12)!

YOUR FAITH GROWS EXCEEDINGLY

In 1 Thessalonians 2:13 Paul said to the church, "... when ye received the Word of God which ye heard of us, ye received it not as the word of men, but as it is in truth, the Word of God...." That is God speaking personally and directly to you. And He said in 2 Thessalonians 1:3, "... your faith groweth exceedingly...."

Once you believe God is talking to you, you will begin to rejoice like you have what you need now. Sometimes when you are at home and the devil comes against your mind through your feelings or circumstances, you must say,

"I live by faith. I walk by faith. I believe that God is talking to me right now, so I'm going to rejoice. Victory is mine! Healing is mine! Prosperity is mine! I receive it by faith."

GOD PERFORMS THINGS FOR YOU

"In the midst of his difficulties, Job said, 'For he performeth the thing that is appointed for me; and many such things are with him.'" -Job 23:14

When you read the last chapter of Job, you will find that the Lord gave him twice as much as he had before. Theologians tell us that Job's trials, as related in the Book of Job, lasted less than a year.

"...In the world ye shall have tribulation [difficulty] but be of good cheer; I have overcome the world."
- John 16:33

Satan is the god of this world. You are not exempt from challenges, but once you know who you are in Christ and Christ is in you, you always overcome. You always come out on top. The Lord said it to me this way, "You will have challenges in life, but you are not the challenger; you are the champion." In boxing, the champion enters the ring with a different attitude than the challenger. The challenger is trying to get something. The champion, on the other hand, says, "I've got something."

GOD'S ABILITY AND OUR RESPONSIBILITY

The spirit of faith actually has two sides — ours and God's. God's ability and our responsibility are the two parts of faith. What is our response to God's ability? Grace is God's grip on you, and faith is your grip on God.

You study faith, you walk by faith, and you live by faith. There are times when it may seem like your faith doesn't have the grip you need. When you sense that, look to the grace of God. Realize that God's grip on you is stronger than your grip on Him!

Even when it seems like your faith is not working, God still has hold of you. The Apostle Paul said, "Not as though I had already attained, either were already perfect...," Philippians 3:12. Another translation says, "I have not gotten hold of what has gotten hold of me."

God performs what He has spoken concerning you. Another aspect of faith is that you don't have to bring it to pass; God brings it to pass.

Dad Hagin says, "You don't have to make it happen; you let it happen." That is why the person who believes has entered into rest (Hebrews 4:3). You cease from your efforts and finally, when you enter into rest, God brings it to pass.

The Bible says that the Lord gives his beloved sleep or rest (Psalm 127:2). God brings it to pass even while you are resting. He performs the things that are appointed to you. Philippians 2:13 says, "For it is God which worketh in you both to will and to do of His good pleasure." God has good things planned for you.

THE END OF YOUR FAITH

Don't fight with your reasoning or your flesh. Don't try to figure everything out. Just say, "I'm going to rest and enjoy. The fight of faith is a good fight."

Some people think they are fighting the fight of faith, but you can tell by their face that even though they may be fighting, they are not fighting the faith fight. They are trying so hard to bring it to pass, they are getting in God's way. When you don't have a spirit of faith, everyone can see what you are going through by your countenance.

Have you ever believed God for something and gotten stuck right in the middle? You have seen the blessing to a degree, and you know there is more ahead, but it seems like you are stuck in the middle.

Peter says, "Let me show you how to get from the believing to the end." Where is the end of your faith? It is when the thing you believe for shows up, and you don't have to believe for it anymore.

To get from believing to receiving — when you have a spirit of faith — you must rejoice with "joy unspeakable and full of glory," 1 Peter 1:8,9. Your faith has an end. This situation you are in has an end! The Amplified Bible says, "...receiving the outcome of your faith."

When you start rejoicing, the glory of God shows up. Then you can laugh, jump, shout, and rejoice because you have seen the outcome of your faith.

FAITH WILL NOT NECESSARILY

PREVENT ALL MOUNTAINS,

BUT IT WILL MOVE THEM!

MARK 11:23

12

MOVE TO MONTANA

CHAPTER TWELVE

Jesus made one of the most amazing statements in the Bible in Mark 9:23, when He said, "...If thou canst believe, all things are possible to him that believeth." With that one statement, Jesus opened the door to the supernatural! He was encouraging us to take the limits off of our lives and enter the realm of God.

We know that with God all things are possible, but Jesus put the believer in the realm of God. We know from Hebrews 11:6 that without faith it is impossible to please God. Faith pleases God and releases His supernatural ability. Unbelief and doubt limit God and stop His power. Faith takes off the limits!

At one time the State of Montana removed speed limits from its highways. During this time a newspaper article reported that a Montana highway patrolman stopped a man for going more than 100 miles per hour. After observing the quality of the man's vehicle and checking his driving record, the patrolman let him off without a ticket. What a place to visit — a place with no limits!

God has given us a quality vehicle in His Word to go beyond the limits of the natural man into the supernatural. Spiritually speaking, some people have never been to "Montana." Some people have only visited there once or twice, and others have decided to move there.

Learn to live everyday believing all things are possible. Someone said that a miracle comes your way every day. Learn to recognize the possibilities of God that surround you. Some people are content to putter through life and simply make their mortgage payments. Others reach out for the impossible and see the supernatural!

I like what Norman Vincent Peale said, "It seems there is an invisible reservoir of abundance in the universe that can be tapped into by obeying certain spiritual laws."

There is no need to be in lack if you learn how to tap into that reservoir. As you learn the laws of God and what pleases Him, abundance will flow to you.

THE LAW OF FAITH

There are a number of universal laws. The one we will discuss here is what the Apostle Paul called "the law of faith," Romans 3:27. God is a faith God. The more we understand about faith, the better we will understand what moves Him.

God demands faith of us. Without faith it is impossible to please Him. Smith Wigglesworth said that God would pass over a million people just to find someone who believes Him.

Faith pleased God in the Old Testament. That is how Abraham received from God and became "the Father of faith." We also see Jesus in the gospels telling the woman with the issue of blood, "Daughter, thy faith hath made thee whole...," Mark 5:34. Faith not only pleased Him; it seems He was looking for it. He told the Roman centurion, "...I have not found so great faith, no, not in Israel," Matthew 8:10.

In the Book of Acts, we find that faith also pleases and moves the Holy Spirit. For example, in Acts 10:19, 20, the Holy Spirit told Peter to go to Caesarea with Cornelius' servants, "doubting nothing." The Holy Spirit was trying to get Peter to take the limits off God.

It takes faith to please God. God the Father, God the

Son, and God the Holy Spirit are pleased by faith. Faith pleased God in both the Old and New Testaments.

In Malachi 3:6, God said, "I am the Lord, I change not...." Faith will please God throughout eternity. Therefore, this "law of faith" is not a temporary law; it is part of the nature of God, and it will last forever.

MOUNTAIN - MOVING FAITH

Learn how to walk by faith. God not only tells us how to get faith, He tells us how faith works.

> "...*Have faith in God. For verily I say unto you, That whosoever shall say unto this mountain, Be thou removed, and be thou cast into the sea; and shall not doubt in his heart, but shall believe that those things which he saith shall come to pass; he shall have whatsoever he saith.*" - Mark 11:22-23

A note in the margin of my Bible indicates that the literal Greek meaning of verse 22 is, "Have the faith of God." If the Lord Jesus said we are to "have" the faith of God, it must be possible to "have" faith. And not only is it possible but it is also necessary and mandatory.

Jesus was saying here in Mark 11 that there will be

times in your life when nothing natural will move the mountain you are facing. It will take the supernatural to move that mountain. It will take the faith of God to open the door to the supernatural and release the power of God.

The God-kind of faith is an absolute necessity in this life; it is not an accessory or an option. If Jesus said to "have" faith, we must need it.

WE HAVE THE SAME SPIRIT OF FAITH

This kind of faith works by believing in your heart and saying with your mouth. Writing under the inspiration of the Holy Spirit to the church at Corinth, the Apostle Paul said,

> *"We having the same spirit of faith, according as it is written, I believed, and therefore have I spoken; we also believe, and therefore speak."*
> *- 2 Corinthians 4:13*

Paul said "we" have the same spirit of faith. I have and you have — we have — the same spirit of faith. We believe and we speak. This is how faith works, by believing and speaking. Notice Paul did not say, "We are trying to get it," he said, "We've got it!"

In Romans 12:3, Paul says that God has dealt to every man "the measure of faith." Every born-again believer has a measure of the God-kind of faith. You have a measure of mountain - moving faith. Your faith can grow and increase by feeding on the Word of God and by exercising it, because we have the same spirit of faith.

Remember, Jesus was not performing a "deity trick" in His teaching in Mark 11. He was not showing off what God could do. If He had, He never would have said, "Whosoever shall say...." This will work for anyone. This is the law of faith that taps into God's reservoir of power and abundance to meet every need of mankind. Thank God for His Word!

Move to "Montana" in your faith. You have a measure of the God-kind of faith, and all things are possible to you, a believer. Take the LIMITS off!

SOME PEOPLE ARE SELF-CONSCIOUS,

SOME PEOPLE ARE

PEOPLE-CONSCIOUS,

SOME PEOPLE ARE UNCONSCIOUS,

BUT WE SHOULD BE GOD-CONSCIOUS.

13

FAITH AIN'T PRETTY
CHAPTER THIRTEEN

A local tire store had an advertisement that caught my attention. The ad said, "Hello, neighbor! Tires ain't pretty, but everyone needs tires, so you might as well get them from us at the best price."

Some time later I was in a radical, wild church service where people were laughing, rejoicing, shouting, and praising God. Some were even leaping for joy, running, and dancing! During all of this, the Lord spoke to me in this way, "Hello, neighbor! Faith ain't pretty, but everyone needs faith! So get your faith from God and learn how to release your faith and respond to the Word and the power of God."

"So then faith cometh by hearing, and hearing by the word of God." - Romans 10:17

"I rejoice at thy word, as one that findeth great spoil." - Psalm 119:162

"Thy words were found, and I did eat them; and thy word was unto me the joy and rejoicing of mine heart...." - Jeremiah 15:16

"...yet believing, ye rejoice with joy unspeakable and full of glory: Receiving the end of your faith, even the salvation of your souls." - 1 Peter 1:8, 9

Notice that between "believing" and "receiving" in these verses is "joy unspeakable."

JOY UNSPEAKABLE

When you are really a Bible believing Christian, there must be some rejoicing with joy unspeakable. If the joy is "unspeakable," you must let it out somehow through laughing, shouting, leaping, or dancing for joy. This kind of joy is full of glory. The spirit of faith declares the outcome even in the middle of adversity. You see the victorious end of the challenge you are facing.

Some people would have great faith, but they are too concerned about being pretty all the time. They want to look cool or sophisticated. Real Bible faith ain't always pretty. (I know that may not be good English, but it is still true.)

SHOUTING, DANCING, AND RUNNING

When the glory of God is manifested, it brings the supernatural power of God. The spirit of faith will cause you to shout while the walls are still standing, like God's people did at Jericho before the walls came down (Joshua 6:20).

The spirit of faith will cause you to dance like David did when the Ark of the Covenant was returned to Jerusalem and the glory returned (2 Samuel 6:14,15). The spirit of faith may cause you to run like Elijah did when the hand of the Lord came upon him (1 Kings 18:46). The rain he had prayed and contended for was coming, and he outran the king's chariot. The spirit of faith will cause you to sing and praise God loudly, as Paul and Silas did at midnight when they were imprisoned in chains (Acts 16:25). The power of God shook the prison and set them free.

These are demonstrations of the power of God, and they are all connected to faith. Everyone needs faith. Romans 1:17 says, "...the just shall live by faith." According to Hebrews 11:6, faith pleases God. Dr. Lilian B. Yeomans said it this way, "God delights in His children stepping out over the aching void with nothing under their feet but the Word of God." God watches as we demonstrate a faith that acts on the Word.

The spirit of faith may often cause a person to look foolish, as Naaman did when the prophet Elisha told him to dip seven times in the muddy Jordan River (2 Kings 5:14). What God required of Naaman for his healing from leprosy was not difficult, but it seemed too foolish. Naaman's reasoning almost made him miss his miracle, but he finally acted on the prophet's word and was totally healed.

"But God hath chosen the foolish things of the world to confound the wise; and God hath chosen the weak things of the world to confound the things which are mighty." - 1 Corinthians 1:27

The answer still is,

"...Not by might, nor by power, but by my spirit, saith the Lord of hosts." - Zechariah 4:6

THE SHOUT OF FAITH

"...I have made thee a father of many nations, before him whom he believed, even God, who quickeneth the dead, and calleth those things which be not as though they were." - Romans 4:17

I like what Smith Wigglesworth said in his book "Ever Increasing Faith" about the shout of faith:

God help us to understand this! It is time people knew how to shout in faith as they contemplate the eternal power of our God, to whom it is nothing to quicken and raise the dead. I come across some people who would be giants in the power of God, but they have no shout of faith. I find everywhere people who fail, even when they are praying, simply because they are just breathing sentences without uttering speech — and you cannot get victory that way. You must learn to take the victory and shout in the face of the devil, "It is done!" Things will be different, and tremendous things will happen.

GET "UGLY" FOR JESUS

Recently I was ministering at a campmeeting with several other ministers. One night, the meeting became particularly radical and unusual. As people were rejoicing and enjoying the presence of God, some looked rather comical. A minister friend of mine said to me, "Those people are not ashamed to get 'ugly' for Jesus!" I laughed and agreed. We rejoiced as people received from God.

Sometimes you have to get "ugly" for Jesus. If you want the anointing and the power of God, you must act like the Bible is true!

The spirit of faith can be seen and heard. Smith Wigglesworth said, "No man can doubt when he learns to shout."

CHANGED BY FAITH

You don't have to be perfect to have a spirit of faith. Some people disqualify themselves from the blessings of God or from being used by God because they think they have too many flaws. While it is true that you are to keep growing spiritually, you do not need to have reached perfection to have a spirit of faith.

The great faith chapter of Hebrews 11 includes many people who were far from perfect. There were flaws in Abraham, Sarah, Noah, Moses, Samson, David, and many others in the Bible who had a spirit of faith.

I am glad that God works with imperfect people. The spirit of faith enables you to overcome in every area of your life. Smith Wigglesworth said, "Any man may be changed by faith, no matter how he may be fettered."

Recently I was talking to a jeweler about diamonds. He said that all diamonds have a flaw somewhere that can be seen by the trained eye using a magnifying glass. However, the fake diamonds we call cubic zirconiums (cz's) are flawless. They are man-made. Although they look like diamonds, they are much cheaper, and they have only a fraction of the value of a real diamond.

You are valuable to God. He sees you in Christ. He will keep working with you if you keep a spirit of faith and seek Him with all your heart. Sometimes the devil will tell you that you are not the real thing, because you have a flaw. I'm sure you do have a flaw, but you are still a real diamond. At least you are not a cubic zirconium! You don't have to be perfect to have a spirit of faith.

The spirit of faith comes in all sizes, colors, and ages. You could be 17, like David was when he killed Goliath, or 80, like Joshua and Caleb were when they entered the

Promised Land. The spirit of faith cannot tell what color your skin is or how much education you have. The spirit of faith cannot tell whether you are handsome or homely.

The spirit of faith has one thing in common — it believes and speaks. The spirit of faith acts on the Word of God.

BELIEVE AND SPEAK

All scripture is inspired by God (2 Timothy 3:16). The word "inspired" means "God-breathed." Jesus said in Matthew 4:4, "...Man shall not live by bread alone, but by every word that proceedeth out of the mouth of God."

The Word of God was spoken before it was written. It proceeded out of the mouth of God. Then it was spoken and written by men for us. It was spoken before it was written, and it was written that it might be spoken. The spirit of faith must believe and speak.

The Word of God in your mouth is God giving you mouth-to-mouth resuscitation. The spoken Word gives the life of God to all who believe and speak.

EVERYONE NEEDS AT LEAST

FOUR "CRAZY" FRIENDS

WHO BELIEVE THAT, WITH GOD,

ALL THINGS ARE POSSIBLE.

LUKE 5

14

JESUS SAW THEIR FAITH

CHAPTER FOURTEEN

"Now faith is...." That's one of the great secrets of faith. God is looking for faith, and He can see when someone gets in the now. Jesus never told anyone to return the next day or in 30 days. In other words, the question is not God's ability. The question is, can you bring your faith into the now? Can you get it on the inside of you in the now — today?

This is the day, now is the time, this is the place, and you are the person. You must say, "I believe I have it now." Once you get into the now, all things are possible with God. Remember, Jesus never told anyone to return the next day.

Faith can be heard and faith can be seen. If you had passed the woman with the issue of blood in the street, you would have heard her faith. She confessed, "...If I may touch but his clothes, I shall be whole," Mark 5:28. You would also have seen her faith, because she would have been moving the best way she could in her weakened, bleeding condition. Her faith caused her to be moving. She could have just stood there and said, "If the Lord wants me to be healed, He'll just have to come to my house." But the Bible says that when she heard of Jesus, she started moving and talking or confessing.

You've got to start moving and talking, too. You've got to do something that seems impossible, and you've got to start declaring or confessing something that seems impossible — something no one but God could do for you.

What kind of a prayer line would we have in meetings today if everyone was like her, and they had already been confessing before prayer, "I know as soon as hands are laid on me, I will receive my healing. I believe I have received my healing! I know it's mine!"

CORPORATE FAITH

You can see individual faith like that possessed by the woman with the issue of blood, and you can also see corporate faith in the gospels. Luke 5:20 says, "When Jesus saw their faith...." Their faith was people joining their faith together. The four men who carried their paralyzed friend to Jesus had corporate faith.

The paralyzed man also had individual faith. Few invalids would have allowed themselves to be carried out of their home as he did, because it was so painful. However, this invalid allowed his friends to take him to the house where Jesus was teaching. When they got there and found the house was filled with people, they all agreed, "Let's go up on the roof. This is it. Today's the day. We're not going home. We're not coming back another day, and we're not going to see if they can make room for us. We're going up on that roof and knocking a hole in it!"

PERMANENT JUBILEE

In Luke 4, Jesus gave His sermon from Isaiah 61 — His sermon on Jubilee. Jesus was trying to bring Jubilee to Nazareth. He is always trying to bring Jubilee. He's the permanent Jubilee!

Jesus always brings healing and deliverance. He endeavors to bless you and give you victory. If you are in bondage or have been held hostage, Jesus wants to set you free.

Jesus was from Nazareth, where He was known as the son of a carpenter. He read Isaiah 61: "The Spirit of the

Lord is upon me. He has anointed me." He was saying, "This is it. I'm the person. Now is the time. What are you going to do about it?" The people of Nazareth doubted Jesus.

Now, in Luke 5, Jesus was in another place teaching the doctors of the Law — men who had memorized the whole Old Testament. These men had doubts about Him, also.

Never be discouraged when you've got a room full of sad-looking and unbelieving faces because someone is on the way to the roof! Someone is always on the way to their miracle.

Just keep saying, "This is it, now is the time, this is the day, and the anointing of the Holy Spirit is here. Someone is going to believe God. Someone is on the way to the roof right now!"

KNOCKING A HOLE FROM THE NATURAL TO THE SUPERNATURAL

Never underestimate the power of an act of faith for you, your family, and your future. I believe that acts of faith are being recorded in what I call "God's Book of Exploits."

This book of remembrance is still being written about you, your family, your city, and your nation. Every time you do something in faith, God says, "Write that down. Get that in the library!" Never underestimate the power of believing God and declaring what He says.

The Lord once showed me a vision of people running, jumping, dancing, and laughing. He showed me people jumping through a hole into the power of God and getting the manifestation of their miracle. I asked, "What is that, Lord?" He said, "That's Luke 5. People have been jumping through the hole those five men knocked from the natural to the supernatural and receiving their miracle for the last 2,000 years."

People have been reading that Bible story and saying, "I believe I can get my miracle. I believe I can knock a hole in the roof and jump through." That hole is big enough for you, your family, your friends, and your city. It's even big enough for a whole nation.

If people do not understand the fight of faith, they also will not understand the peace and the tranquility that fills your heart once you've knocked your hole in the roof and sat at the feet of Jesus. Whatever it takes, get to the feet of Jesus! Once you get there, everything will be all right.

REAL BIBLE FAITH

Often we want faith to be easy. Do you think the devil is going to let you say faith confessions without coming around and attacking you? You may have said a few things on the way to the house, but you wouldn't go up on the roof because you were too embarrassed and didn't want to face the pain. Go ahead — go onto the roof and let them knock a hole in it for you.

Real Bible faith doesn't get embarrassed. It is not timid and is not self-conscious or conscious of people. Real Bible faith says, "This is it — Jesus and me — now! I'm not doing this to impress anyone. I'm not trying to show anyone how spiritual I am. I need something from Jesus that I know I can't get any other way."

JESUS IS LOOKING FOR FAITH

You need to knock a hole in your roof. If you've got a body, you've got authority in the earth. If you've got a voice, you've got authority in the earth. Can you move? Good. Jesus can work with you. All He is looking for is faith.

Jesus was a great faith preacher. While He was teaching, the atmosphere got charged with faith because of the Word of God. Everything you can see was created by the Word of God. Faith is the material that makes up everything. Faith itself is made up of two major parts — believing and speaking.

When faith starts believing and speaking, it starts acting like what it's believing and speaking. It starts moving in that direction. Your body may shake with fear, but your spirit will move. When Jesus saw the faith of the sick man and his friends, He recognized that it was corporate faith.

There is a fight to faith. The faith walk is not necessarily the easiest road. It's a challenging road, but it's also a glory road. If you believe, you'll see the glory, like the paralyzed man did.

Luke 5:20 records, "When he [Jesus] saw their faith, he said unto him, Man, thy sins are forgiven thee." Jesus was doing faith surgery. The scribes and the Pharisees were shocked, and Jesus knew what they were thinking.

> *"...What reason ye in your hearts? Whether is easier, to say, Thy sins be forgiven thee; or to say, Rise up and walk? But that ye may know that the Son of man hath power upon earth to forgive sins, (he said unto the sick of the palsy,) I say unto thee,*

> *Arise, and take up thy couch, and go into thine house. And immediately he rose up before them, and took up that whereon he lay, and departed to his own house, glorifying God. And they were all amazed, and they glorified God, and were filled with fear, saying, We have seen strange things to day."* - Luke 5:22-26

As Jesus told the doctors of the Law, His ability was not the issue. He had the willingness and the power to forgive sins and to heal the sick. Furthermore, all things are possible to the person who believes.

LIVING BY FAITH

Living by faith is different from trying to use your faith every once in a while. Living by faith means getting up in the morning and choosing to walk by faith, not by sight. Then, in the afternoon, when you have an opportunity to declare the way you feel or the way things look, you've got to say what God says.

Smith Wigglesworth said, "God has designed that the just shall live by faith." God designed it this way. Dad Hagin didn't make this up, Smith Wigglesworth didn't make this up and Oral Roberts didn't make this up. This didn't come out of Tulsa; it came out of Nazareth! God has designed that the just shall live by faith.

I carry the book ***Ever Increasing Faith*** by Smith Wigglesworth with me everywhere I go. Once I've read it through, I start reading it again. I continually want to find out more about his faith walk. He raised 24 people from the dead, and was also a prosperous man. When he went into the ministry, he told the Lord, "I'll always wear the best."

Your faith will work wherever you turn it, but you've got to get it focused on something, and you've got to have confidence. God is arranging things and putting them within the reach of your faith. However, sometimes there is a stretch of water that has to be walked on before you get your miracle.

The scribes and the Pharisees admitted they had seen strange things that day. God wants to do some strange things in our day, too. Of course, these things will not seem strange to those of us who know the Bible.

We live by faith, we walk by faith, and we fight the good fight of faith. We hold fast to our confession of faith. We know all things are possible to those who believe.

Jesus is looking for faith. In Luke 8:18, Jesus asked, "...when the Son of man cometh, shall he find faith on the earth?" It takes faith to move with God. It takes faith to obey God. It takes faith to please God. Confess right now:

I have a measure of the God-kind of faith, and that measure is growing. I believe and I speak. I have overcoming faith — mountain-moving faith.

> *"...whosoever shall say unto this mountain, Be thou removed, and be thou cast into the sea; and shall not doubt in his heart, but shall believe that those things which he saith..." - Mark 11:23*

I have the same kind of faith that created the world in the beginning. I have a measure of the God-kind of faith, and it's framing my world with blessing, healing, victory, and prosperity. I believe and I speak!

THE WORD OF GOD WAS SPOKEN

BEFORE IT WAS WRITTEN, AND IT WAS

WRITTEN SO IT COULD BE SPOKEN.

2 PETER 1:21

15

GROWING FAITH

CHAPTER FIFTEEN

In the book, ***Ever Increasing Faith***, Smith Wigglesworth is quoted as having said many profound things about faith. Two major areas in the book are living by faith and being filled with the Holy Spirit.

As you study the Book of Acts, you'll find the people were full of faith and the Holy Spirit. Those two things are really important. If you are expecting miracles, you must learn how to walk by faith and be filled with the Spirit. God is raising up men and women like this today.

I believe Smith Wigglesworth was an apostle of faith. If you are serious about walking and living by faith, you must study not only the Word of God, but also the lives of men and women God has anointed to be apostles, prophets, evangelists, pastors, and teachers. God has anointed them to speak the Word of God and to write the word of faith to this generation.

The Lord said it to me this way, "You've got to get it before you get it. Once you get it, you'll get it. Once you get it, you'll act like you've got it. Then, once you've got it, you can say, 'I've got it. I'm not trying to get it, I don't hope to get it. I've got it.'"

> *"...What things soever ye desire, when ye pray, believe that ye receive them, and ye shall have them."*
> *- Mark 11:24*

> *"For whosoever hath, to him shall be given, and he shall have more abundance: but whosoever hath not, from him shall be taken away even that he hath." - Matthew 13:12*

Once you get faith for it on the inside, you'll get it on the outside. Now faith is. Believe God.

As we saw earlier, Dr. Lilian B. Yeomans commented, "God delights in His children stepping out over the aching void with nothing under their feet but the Word of God." When I read that statement, the first thing I thought about was someone stepping over a cliff with nothing under their feet but the Word of God. The second thing I thought about was the statement, "God delights." I wonder what makes Him so happy? I believe that, because He is a faith God, everything is created by faith. I believe we will have to exercise our faith throughout eternity, and things will be created with faith.

I believe God delights over His children, like we delight when our children first crawl and then take steps. I believe God is just like that. As our Daddy, He is saying, "Come on, let Me show you how I walk. Let Me show you how things work. Let Me show you how to receive. Let Me show you how to be blessed." When you start to take little steps, I believe He smiles and says, "Look at him! Look at that!"

The devil will do everything he can to get you in the sense realm or the feeling realm. When this happens, simply say, "I'm not going." Dad Hagin said, "If the devil can get you out of the arena of faith, he'll whip you. If he can get you into the arena of sight, feelings, and circumstances, he'll whip you every time." Make the devil come into the arena of faith; that is where you always win!

CLEARED FOR 40,000 FEET

I like the way one preacher described growing faith. As he was taking off in his jet one day, the control tower said, "You're cleared for 10,000 feet." The plane rose to 10,000 feet. After a while, the control tower said, "You're cleared for 20,000 feet." The preacher flew up to 20,000 feet. Then the tower said, "You're cleared for 40,000 feet," so he went up to 40,000 feet. You can't say, "I'm going to fly wherever I want to." The man in the control tower knows things you don't know.

Likewise, Jesus is the Author and the Finisher of your faith. Faith is obeying God. You must wait until you've got clearance to climb to higher spiritual altitudes.

My preacher friend said that while he was climbing higher, the Lord spoke to him, saying, "I wish you had as much confidence in Me as you do in that man in the control tower. When I tell you that you are cleared for 20,000 feet, pull the throttle back and head for it."

You know when you are cleared in your spirit. When you have the spirit of faith, you know how your faith works. You've already exercised your faith, and you know if something is troubling you, you'd better stay at 20,000 feet until something on the inside of you — the Holy Spirit

— says that you are cleared for 40,000 feet. When He says you are, just pull the throttle back and let your faith grow.

THE SPIRIT OF FAITH

WILL ANNOUNCE THE OUTCOME

IN THE MIDDLE

OF THE ADVERSITY.

16
FAITH CHALLENGES
CHAPTER SIXTEEN

Most people do not understand the challenge of the fight of faith. Jesus told the Syrophoenician woman who came to Him pleading for her daughter's healing, "Let the children first be filled....," Mark 7:27-29. Jesus wanted to heal her daughter, but He recognized she didn't have the faith to receive it. So He just stopped and kept working on her to see if her faith could come up a notch. When it did, He said, "It's done. Your daughter is healed!" Dr. Lilian B. Yeomans said He was really doing surgery on her faith!

It's easy to talk faith and learn all of the right confessions until you face challenges in your life. Some people claim, "I'm trying God." But God can't be tried; He is already proven. Sometimes your faith may be tested by God or circumstances. God can always take the simplest thing, help you receive it, and take you up another notch in your faith.

YOUR FAITH WORKS ANYTIME

Your walk of faith may run through stormy waters. "Few people understand except those who have battled the fierce waves and the darkness of the night, and the difficulty," one faith pioneer noted. When Peter walked on the water (Matthew 14:25-33), it seemed as if the Lord picked the worst time. It was 3 o'clock in the morning, the waves were high, and the winds were blowing when Jesus came walking toward the disciples over the water.

Peter asked, "Lord, is that You? I want to come to You." Jesus said, "Come"— one word. He didn't say, "Come on, you can do it!" People criticize Peter for sinking, but they forget he's the only one who got out of the boat!

It seems as if God always picks the time when it looks like you're the weakest and you can't do it. Peter could have said, "Lord, could we try this tomorrow afternoon?" People always have suggestions for God. What He wants to do doesn't fit into their schedule at the time. But God picks that time to show that faith in Him will work anytime, anywhere, and for anyone who will believe Him.

ANNOUNCE THE OUTCOME
IN THE MIDDLE OF THE BATTLE

*"Wherefore, sirs, be of good cheer: for I believe
God, that it shall be even as it was told me."*
- Acts 27:25

I like the Apostle Paul's attitude in the middle of a storm. He didn't say he wasn't having a storm. He simply said, "I'm going over, I'm not going under. There might be a storm, but I believe God, and everything is going to be all right." That takes a spirit of faith. Some people like to brag about how much they believed during the storm after they arrive safely on the shore. "I tell you, I knew everything was going to be all right, Pastor." Where were they when all the others on board were hanging over the side of the boat, throwing up and moaning, "We're all going to die in this storm!"

The spirit of faith will announce the outcome in the middle of the battle - in the middle of the trial - in the middle of the struggle - in the middle of the challenge. The spirit of faith will say, "I'm getting happy right now, because I have a Word from God. God said, 'Everything is going to be all right.' I believe God and it shall be even as He told me."

PERFORMANCE OF YOUR FAITH

Dr. Lilian B. Yeomans, a medical doctor, wrote that when she was dying of drug addiction, another woman, who was dying of cancer, was with her.

When I was addicted to morphine and at my last gasp, I had a lovely friend, a beautiful woman, cultured, wealthy, and, most important, deeply spiritual. She lived in her Bible and lived it out in her daily life....She and I had a strange experience that drew us very close together. We were dying at the same time, she of a malignant growth, I of morphine addiction, hopeless cases both of them. We used to sit together "beside the silent sea," waiting the sound of "the muffled oar" with our Bibles open in front of us. As we turned the leaves we found them "leaves of healing," for there was divine healing on every page. But we could not seem to grasp it, for there was a stretch of water to be walked upon. How to take the leap? Yet it must be done if we were to survive. We were not afraid to go, and yet we felt as though we ought to be healed in view of God's promises. At last I somehow got out of the boat and walked on the water. I think God had to make it nearly capsize to get me out. When I saw the waves boisterous and I sank, He caught me. By this time my lovely friend had been taken by her devoted husband to some sanitarium where, though I tried my best, I could not reach her. I never saw her again....Then I heard that Voice. He said, "Walk on the water. You have been looking for improvements in symptoms, a change in the natural order of things. Stop it. That isn't it at all. My word is absolutely true. My healing is supernatural. It doesn't matter how you feel. Step out." And I did.

Faith says, "I believe I have it." The "performance department" is God's department. In other words, your department is to stand on the Word, keep your eyes and expectation on Jesus, and keep moving.

Smith Wigglesworth said it this way, "There have been times when I have been pressed through circumstances and it seemed as if a dozen railroad engines were going over me. But I have found that the hardest things are just lifting places into the grace of God. We have such a lovely Jesus. He always proves himself to be such a mighty deliverer. He never fails to plan the best things for us." I'm so glad Smith Wigglesworth said that, because years later people can read it when they are crying out in the midst of difficulties and challenges.

CRY OUT FOR JESUS

When you hang out around faith people, you'll hear cries every now and then of, "Jesus, help me!" The ministry of Jesus was like that. People were hollering to Him all the time. In Matthew 15:22, the Syrophoenician woman hollered. Blind Bartimaeus cried out for mercy in Mark 10:48. Peter said in Matthew 14:30, "Lord, save me!" The only people who hollered were people who believed God but needed to make an adjustment in their faith.

If you begin to sink and don't know what to do, you can cry and say, "Lord, what am I doing wrong?" Some people would rather sink than ask the Lord what they are doing wrong. I'd rather ask Him what I am doing wrong.

The other disciples were scared when they saw Peter get out of the boat and walk on the water. Sometimes a stretch of water must be walked on before you can get to Jesus for the miracle you need.

DON'T DESPISE THE DAY
OF SMALL BEGINNINGS

Some people think they can bypass walking by faith. They think, "That's really good for those faith people — if you're in that camp." But there is only one camp — God the Father of glory and the Father of our Lord Jesus Christ.

He is a faith God. Whatever denomination you are in, you might as well learn this: The just shall live by faith!

Jesus is looking for faith. You can use your faith and go from riding a bicycle to owning a really nice car. Then you can say, "Look what the Lord provided for me as I used my faith." Don't be embarrassed about that. The Bible says not to despise the day of small beginnings. God wants you to have nice things, because you represent Him. You're an ambassador for the Lord Jesus Christ.

So don't sit back and say, "I wish I didn't have these challenges." It may not look like it or feel like it, but it shall be as He told you. You have the Word on it. You are not moved by feelings or impressions; you are only moved by the Word.

NO MAN LOOKS AT APPEARANCES IF

HE BELIEVES GOD. I'M NOT MOVED BY

WHAT I SEE. I'M NOT MOVED BY WHAT

I FEEL. I'M MOVED ONLY BY WHAT I

BELIEVE AND I BELIEVE IN GOD!

-SMITH WIGGLESWORTH

17

FAITH CAN BE SEEN
CHAPTER SEVENTEEN

God not only demands faith of us, but He has provided the means whereby we can get faith.

> *"So then faith cometh by hearing, and hearing by the word of God." - Romans 10:17*

God's Word is "faith food." When faith cometh, fear goeth, and the devil runneth. Faith brings God's power on the scene. God is looking for faith. We know that faith pleases Him.

"For the eyes of the Lord run to and fro throughout
the whole earth, to show himself strong in the behalf
of them whose heart is perfect toward him...."
- 2 Chronicles 16:9

One way you can act on your faith is to start believing and saying the same thing God says. Another way you can act on the Word of God is to start releasing your faith. Act like it's true! Smith Wigglesworth said, "No man looks at appearances if he believes God. I'm not moved by what I see. I'm not moved by what I feel. I'm moved by what I believe, and I believe God." Faith moves you to act on the Word of God.

FOUR CRAZY FRIENDS

In Luke 5:20, when the paralyzed man was healed, Jesus saw the faith of his friends. At that time, Jesus was teaching an educated crowd — Pharisees and doctors of the Law. The Bible says the power of God was present to heal, but none of them got healed.

At the end of Luke 5, the Bible says these educated men went away amazed. When you believe God and receive your victory, even your critics will admit, "Something is going on in their life." Dr. Lilian B. Yeomans explained in her book, **The Great Physician**, that a cluster of diamonds has a brilliance that a solitaire never has. In other words, diamonds are most effectively displayed on a black background. The darker the background, the more brilliant the diamonds. In His encounter with the doctors of the Law, Jesus was teaching in the midst of the darkest, most determined unbelief — and it was not an individual's unbelief; it was national, corporate unbelief.

These doctors of the Law had come from every city and village throughout the whole region to criticize Jesus. However, in the middle of their most persistent, educated unbelief, five flashing "faith diamonds" came through the roof. Everyone needs at least four crazy friends who will believe that God can do anything — and now is the time for Him to do it!

"When Jesus saw their faith...." The Bible doesn't say He was looking for their luxury car. It doesn't say He saw how nicely they were dressed. It doesn't say He saw their stylish hairdos or how much education they had. He was looking for faith.

When some people get blessed, they think they can quit living by faith. No, the just will always live by faith. Even after you get your nice car, your jet, your big house, and after all your family is saved - you still must live by faith. Living by faith is not something you do every once in a while; it's a daily walk with God.

FAITH COMES BY HEARING & HEARING

In Acts 14, they perceived that a crippled man had faith to be healed.

> *"And there they preached the gospel. And there sat a certain man at Lystra, impotent in his feet, being cripple from his mother's womb, who never had walked: The same heard Paul speak: who steadfastly beholding him, and perceiving that he had faith to be healed, Said with a loud voice, Stand upright on thy feet. And he leaped and walked."*
> *- Acts 14:7-10*

Faith comes by hearing and hearing by the Word of God. While Paul was preaching the Gospel, the man had faith to be healed. Paul was preaching from Luke 4:18-19, Jesus not only died for our sins, but He took our sicknesses and diseases. He also took our poverty, shame, guilt, and depression. This was the same anointing Jesus had, except now because Jesus died and was raised from the dead, His power had been released toward believers.

Paul saw that the crippled man had faith to be healed and it kept him in the realm of faith. Before the man could think about it, Paul said, "Stand up on your feet!" The crippled man shouted, leaped, and walked!

RELEASE YOUR FAITH

James 2:17 says to release your faith; act on your faith. That man could have started thinking, "If I could stand up on my feet, I wouldn't be sitting here right now." Reasoning and unbelief will keep you out of God's best blessings.

Some people disguise unbelief as wisdom. Your intelligence will see no mighty work. They say, "The intelligent thing to do is...."

Some people are afraid to "lose their minds," to let go of their own thinking, opinions, and traditions. They are afraid to let go and let God have His way. "Lose your mind" and get the mind of Christ, the mind of the Anointed One and His anointing.

GOD'S RADAR SCREEN

I believe that God has a radar screen in heaven that only shows faith. He is like an air traffic controller. He can see incoming faith, the location and the movement of faith.

When your faith is in action, it shows up on God's radar screen, and He releases His power to you.

Whenever God finds faith, He can do miracles. Mountains will be removed, sickness will leave, demons will flee, and creative power will be released. When patience is mixed with your faith, it keeps you on target and keeps you in the air until you get to the landing strip where you receive.

Do you want to be on God's giant radar screen? He's looking for people to get in faith by believing the Word, speaking the Word, walking by faith, praising Him, thanking Him for His Word, and holding fast to their confession of faith. When you do that, you will show up on that radar screen and the Father will say, "Faith incoming!"

Faith has to land before it gets the miracle. As we saw in Romans 10:17, "So then faith cometh by hearing, and hearing by the Word of God." I like to say, when faith comes, you know it. When faith comes, something happens in your inner man.

> *"The Lord will light my candle."*
> *- Psalm 18:28*

When He lights your candle, you can run through a troop and leap over a wall (verse 29). There is no problem outside of you that one light, the fire of the Word of God in your inner man, cannot handle. You can run through that troop, jump over that wall, and move that mountain!

At times, people that appear on God's "faith radar screen," do well, and come in for a landing — the manifestation of God's promise. But all of a sudden something happens, and they go off the screen. Doubt or fear came in, and the devil said, "How do you feel? How do things look? Do you think you're ever going to be different? Do you think things will ever change for you? Do you think you'll ever do what God has called you to do? Do you think you'll ever get your healing?"

When this happens, you get out of the spirit and into your thinking, reasoning, and into your sight. You go off the radar screen, and God the Father says, "Oh my, we've got a crash here somewhere. They went off the screen. Someone go and find them!" Someone find them and get them back into believing God and speaking the Word. Then they come back on the screen. Some people stay on the screen for several days at a time, but they go off the screen as soon as the devil attacks them. God wants you to stay on the screen.

Every morning as soon as you get up, you ought to show up on that radar screen. You get on God's radar screen by speaking words of faith, "The Lord is my shepherd, I shall not want. The Lord is my light and my salvation; whom shall I fear? The Lord is the strength of my life." By simply speaking the Word you are back on the screen.

Jesus is always looking for faith. You may wonder, "What is faith?" The palsied man's friends spoke words of faith, "This is it. Now is the time. We believe. This is the day. All we've got to do is get in the presence of Jesus." Jesus saw their faith. He is still looking for faith today, but not yesterday's faith. He is asking, "What do you believe today? What are you declaring today? What are you acting on today?"

FAITH IS

A TEAM SPORT.

LUKE 5

18

CORPORATE FAITH

CHAPTER EIGHTEEN

In Luke 5, when the palsied man's friends lowered him through the roof, Jesus saw corporate faith in action. That's the power of believers pulling together. If you can get believers pulling together in church, faith will be stronger than unbelief.

Faith is what Jesus was looking for. I believe He said, "I only need 12 believers." Once He got the 12 disciples, He went for 70 more. God is always on the increase. When Jesus had the 70, He believed for 120 believers to come together, and they did, in the Upper Room.

Smith Wigglesworth said that it is always a trap of the devil to try to make you independent. We need one another, and we need to submit to one another. This is corporate faith.

The Apostle Paul was glad that a few disciples were holding the ropes of the basket when he was being lowered over the Damascus town wall, escaping persecution (Acts 9:25). Later, he was more important than they were, but at that moment, they were more important than he was.

While holding the ropes, they probably thought they'd like to do something significant for the Lord someday, but perhaps helping Paul escape was the most significant thing they ever did. They were holding in a basket the man who went on to write more than half the New Testament. We need one another, but if the devil can trick you into being independent, he can get you out of a place of faith. Corporate faith is the way God has chosen for us to help one another. We dare not be independent.

God wants to bring us to a place where we submit ourselves to one another. If we refuse, we will get away from the Word of God and out of the place of faith.

FAITH FRIENDS

Smith Wigglesworth said, "I went to a meeting one time and I was very, very sick and got worse. I knew the perfect will of God was for me to humble myself and ask the elders to pray for me. I put it off and the meeting finished. I went home without being anointed and prayed with. Everyone in the house caught the illness I had."

We dare not be independent. Never get so proud of your faith that you think that you don't need any faith help. When your faith wavers, you have faith friends who will encourage you. I thank God for faith friends. Most of us are alive because of faith friends, people who kept believing God and kept believing in us when we didn't even believe in ourselves.

God has great things planned for you and they're just ahead. The devil is trying to get you to stop one step before your miracle.

The people I hang around with have wet sandals. That means they got out of the boat. That means when they began to sink, Jesus pulled them up.

The Church of the Lord Jesus Christ — the Body of Christ — with all its imperfections is still the best place in the whole world to be. You might find a lot of things wrong with the Church, but it's still the best place to be. Don't allow the devil to make you independent.

Make this confession: "I've got faith friends and I'm hanging out with them. They're not perfect friends, but God is working on them just like He's working on me."

YOU ARE

THE BELIEVER

AND GOD IS

THE PERFORMER.

19

JUBILEE FAITH
CHAPTER NINETEEN

Jesus began his earthly ministry when He gave His first message in the synagogue at Nazareth.

> *"The Spirit of the Lord is upon me, because he hath anointed me to preach the gospel to the poor; he hath sent me to heal the brokenhearted, to preach deliverance to the captives, and recovering of sight to the blind, to set at liberty them that are bruised, To preach the acceptable year of the Lord. And he closed the book, and he gave it again to the minister, and sat down. And the eyes of all them that were in the synagogue were fastened on him. And he began to say unto them, This day is this scripture fulfilled in your ears." - Luke 4:18-21*

Jesus was reading from Isaiah 61. He was saying, "Isaiah said this and he was talking about Me. I'm the person. I'm the Messiah, the Anointed One. Now is the time, and this is it. Today I'm preaching the acceptable year of the Lord." The Amplified Bible translates this, "The year when salvation and the free favors of God will profusely abound." Jesus was really talking about the Year of Jubilee, when the Messiah would come and announce, "This is the Year of Jubilee!"

Leviticus 25 explains in detail all the events that happened in a Year of Jubilee. Every fiftieth year, God declared a Year of Jubilee, a year of celebration in the nation of Israel. Jubilee was the year when debts were canceled. Anything you had lost (houses, lands, furniture, anything) had to come back to you. It was the year of righteousness. It was also the year of supernatural increase. God said, "What you plant this year will be so blessed, you'll have an increase that will last for three years."

JUBILEE IS SUPERNATURAL

Jubilee was an unusual time. Every fiftieth year God said, "It's a Year of Jubilee, and I'm changing the whole economy." This means, God can actually afford to tell the economy to do whatever He wants it to do.

God said, "In this fiftieth year, if you've been bound, you go free. If you're in debt, you go free. If you've lost your land, it's got to come back to you. It's a time of Jubilee, a time of celebration, a happy time."

Jesus added financial prosperity to Jubilee. Jubilee is supernatural debt cancellation, supernatural blessing, and supernatural increase that cannot be fully explained in the natural.

In the gospels, we see Jesus operating in signs and wonders when it came to material things. Signs and wonders made it possible for Him to use five loaves and two fishes to feed 5,000 people. Signs and wonders made it possible for Him to catch a fish and pay His taxes with the coin that was in its mouth.

The supernatural is the added ingredient in Jubilee. Jesus gave the first ingredient when He announced, "Now is the time!" The second ingredient is the anointing of the Holy Spirit. The Spirit of God will come upon you to perform it. The third ingredient is the message you see in the Gospel. However, you must mix faith with the Word of God to have your Jubilee.

FREEDOM FROM SICKNESS
AND POVERTY

After Jesus announced the beginning of Jubilee and financial prosperity, He added freedom from sickness.

> *"How God anointed Jesus of Nazareth with the Holy Ghost and with power: who went about doing good, and healing all that were oppressed of the devil; for God was with him." - Acts 10:38*

Sickness is satanic oppression; it is not from God. God anointed Jesus with the Holy Ghost and power, and He went about doing good and healing all. Is it God's will to heal all? Yes, because Jesus went about doing good and healing all.

> *"When the even was come, they brought unto him many that were possessed with devils: and he cast out the spirits with his word, and healed all that were sick." - Matthew 8:16*

This means there is no case too hard for Him to heal. The devil can't come up with a case that is too difficult for Jesus. From the top of your head to the soles of your feet, Jesus is a specialist in all areas of internal and external medicine. He has the cure for your body and your life. He is the cure!

God anointed Jesus with the Holy Spirit and power. Since He was pronouncing a year of Jubilee, it would seem like everyone in Nazareth would have understood and accepted it, and everyone in the vicinity of Jesus would have received miracles.

However, we can see from reading Luke 4 that everyone in Nazareth didn't get it, and they didn't receive miracles. They didn't receive the supernatural debt cancellation, healing, and freedom from oppression.

THE ANOINTING FOLLOWS FAITH

In His sermon in Nazareth, Jesus spoke of the brokenhearted. He was referring to people who had been broken by life, disappointed, hurt, and their lives were left in chaos.

Did you know the anointing is smart? It will go right to the point of your need. Once you learn how to use your faith, the anointing will follow the line of faith. The Jubilee anointing, Jesus' anointing, always follows the line of faith. Jesus' anointing or Jubilee comes where there is faith. People can be in the vicinity of Jubilee anointing and never receive anything. They can be in the vicinity of the power of God in operation and never receive anything. You must exercise faith to receive because God is a faith God.

As Smith Wigglesworth said, "It seems like God will pass over a million people just to find somebody who believes Him." Wouldn't you be disappointed if God passed over you and blessed someone next to you? That would really be sad. God is always trying to find someone who will believe Him.

Remember when Jesus asked, "...when the Son of man cometh, shall he find faith on the earth?" The reason Jesus said that is because faith is the first thing He looks for.

IF YOU DON'T SEE ANY GLORY,

YOU HAD BETTER CHECK YOUR

"BELIEVER," BECAUSE IF YOU DO

BELIEVE, YOU WILL SEE THE GLORY.

JOHN 11:40

20

FAITH RELEASES POWER

CHAPTER TWENTY

The Apostle Paul prayed powerful prayers that were full of faith. One of the best known of these prayers is found in the first chapter of Ephesians.

> *"That the God of our Lord Jesus Christ, the Father of glory, may give unto you the spirit of wisdom and revelation in the knowledge of him: The eyes of your understanding being enlightened; that ye may know what is the hope of his calling, and what the riches of the glory of his inheritance in the saints, And what is the exceeding greatness of his power to usward who believe, according to the working of his mighty power, Which he wrought in Christ, when*

> *he raised him from the dead, and set him at his own*
> *right hand in the heavenly places."*
> *- Ephesians 1:17-20*

Did you notice what Paul said about the "exceeding greatness" of God's power? It is released to us who believe, according to the working of His mighty power that He wrought in Christ when He raised Him from the dead. In other words, the power of God is released toward believers - doubters get nothing.

God's power is "exceeding" great power. People who have heard about it and know the Gospel will say, "I know Jesus has power. I also know the Gospel is the power of God and God is a mighty God." What they don't know is that this power only works toward believers. The power of God follows a line of faith.

Paul said, "It's the same power that raised Christ from the dead." Whatever that power did when it raised Christ from the dead, it will do the same thing in your spirit, your soul, and your body. It will do everything in your body except give you an immortal or glorified body because you will get that at the rapture. God has released enough power to heal you and to drive sickness out of your body. Exceeding great power, unlimited power, is released toward the believer.

CHECK YOUR "BELIEVER"

The power of God could be present, but if you are not a believer or if you don't have your switch of faith turned on, you won't get a thing. People do have such a switch, but they often do not know where it is or how to turn it on.

The power of God is released toward believers. If you have been saying, "I don't ever feel any power, I don't see any mountains moving; I don't see anything changing in my life," you'd better check your "believer" and see how it is doing.

If you are born again, the Bible calls you a believer. Whoever heard of an unbelieving believer? If you are a believer, go ahead and believe. Since I'm a believer, I go ahead and believe God. I believe the Bible. I believe Jesus is alive. I believe the same power that raised Him from the dead is working right now.

Someone said it this way, "Religion worships God for what He did while it fights what He's doing." In other words, religion always wants to discuss the God of the past — the God of the Old Testament or the God of the days of Jesus.

Religious people say, "If only I had been there when Jesus walked the shore of the Sea of Galilee. If only I had been there to see those miracles!" These religious people would probably have been listed in Luke 5 as those who sat there and didn't do anything. They would have been those who were well versed in the scriptures but looked at Jesus and said, "I don't know....He might not be it, and this might not be the day. The power might not be present. I might get it, but I might not get it."

They would have been sitting there as spectators, like the Pharisees and the doctors of the Law, full of head knowledge, not realizing that Jesus, the power of God, was standing right in front of them.

SEE THE GLORY OF GOD

The Messiah was standing right in front of them. Jubilee was standing right in front of them. Healing was standing right in front of them. Deliverance was standing right in front of them. Everything the Old Testament had prophesied about the Messiah was standing right in front of them that day.

Jesus said, "They missed the day of their visitation." God was doing something significant, and the doctors of the Law totally missed it!

Jesus said in John 11:40, "If you believe, you will see the glory of God." If you don't see any glory, you had better check your "believer," because if you do believe, you will see the glory.

The glory is the manifested presence of God. It is present not simply to give you goosebumps but to change things in your life, move mountains, heal your body, cancel your debts, bless you abundantly, bring Jubilee to you, and make you happy.

FAITH PLEASES GOD

Some people say, "I don't think all that faith business is important." Hebrews 11:6 says, "But without faith it is impossible to please him: for he that cometh to God must believe that he is, and that he is a rewarder of them that diligently seek him."

Without faith it is impossible to please God. God is a faith God. You will be frustrated with Him if you don't understand that He is a faith God, and He is looking for faith. God was a faith God in the Old Testament. Jesus in the New Testament is "God with us," and He is looking for faith.

Jesus told the woman with the issue of blood, "... Daughter, thy faith hath made thee whole...," Mark 5:34. Notice He didn't say, "Daughter, my great power, my anointing, and the Jubilee has made you whole." No, He said, daughter, thy faith hath made thee whole. It was this woman's faith that activated the Jubilee, the anointing, and the power.

FAITH WITHOUT

CORRESPONDING ACTION

IS DEAD.

JAMES 2:17-20

21

MIGHTY MIRACLES
REQUIRE FAITH
CHAPTER TWENTY ONE

We know God is able to do all things. Nothing is impossible with God! We also know that God cannot lie. People often say, "It's up to God. If God wants to do it, God can do anything. He's a sovereign God." Apparently, Jesus didn't know that. If God can do anything anytime He wants to, why didn't Jesus do it right there in His own hometown?

Mark 6:5,6 says, "And he could there do no mighty work, save that he laid his hands upon a few sick folk, and healed them. And he marveled because of their unbelief. And he went round about the villages, teaching."

Imagine Jesus being frustrated because He wanted to do a mighty work, but He couldn't? The original Greek implies that He tried, but He couldn't. What is a mighty work? A mighty work is a demonstration of God's power and His glory. Jesus wanted to do something great, a mighty work, but He couldn't. He did lay hands on a few sickly people. Other translations call them, "people with minor ailments."

I believe Jesus wanted to do some mighty Jubilee miracles, mighty demonstrations of His power, but because of unbelief, He couldn't do any mighty work. I wonder what He would say about us today?

TWO KINDS OF UNBELIEF

In Mark 6:6 Jesus marveled because of their unbelief. Then He said, "I've never seen such unbelief." He knew the cure for their unbelief was for Him to go to their cities and villages and teach.

There are two kinds of unbelief. The first is simply ignorance of the Word. This is when people don't know how faith works or that Jesus is the Anointed One. They don't know believing requires a confession and faith requires action. The cure for ignorance is teaching, so Jesus went to all the surrounding cities and villages, and taught the people.

He said, "The Spirit of the Lord is upon Me. He has anointed Me and this is the year of Jubilee. It is time for you to go free. Healing belongs to you, you can also be healed of a broken heart. You can be blessed coming in and going out and be out of debt. This is the time of blessing. This is it! You can get the anointing from Me, but you need to get it right now. Today the scripture is fulfilled in your ears."

As we have seen, the cure for ignorance is found in Romans 10:17, "Faith cometh by hearing, and hearing by the word of God." Jesus went about teaching the Word and curing this kind of unbelief.

Whatever you need faith for, the Bible has the answer. Someone said it this way: "The whole Bible is not about faith, but the whole Bible does have the capacity to produce faith for whatever you need to receive from God." Whether you need salvation, the baptism in the Holy Spirit, divine healing, financial blessing, restoration in your marriage or your family, or whatever else you may need — the answer is already written in the Word.

The faith of someone who believes will cause a beam of light to pierce through unbelief all the way up to heaven, and the anointing will follow that line of faith back to earth and release the power of God.

EDUCATED UNBELIEF

The second kind of unbelief is what the Pharisees and the doctors of the Law showed in Luke 5 — they were unpersuaded to act on the Word of God, they had educated unbelief.

When I talk with people like this, they already know the counsel I'm going to give them and can quote scriptures and references. When I give them a scripture, they'll say, "I know that, Pastor, but you don't understand my problem." No matter how long I counsel them, I can't help them. Although they have been in church and Sunday School for years, they have not been persuaded to act like the Bible is true.

Faith is simply an act. Faith is acting on the Word of God. Faith says, "I believe the Word and I'm acting on it. I'm saying what it says and acting like the Bible is true." That's all faith is — being persuaded to act on the Word of God. James 2:17 says that faith without works is dead. Faith without corresponding action is dead.

Some people do have a form of faith - dead faith. You have to carry dead faith, but living faith will carry you. Some people have all kinds of props trying to support their faith, but living faith will prop you up.

SMALL PROBLEM, BIG GOD

When the problems of life come, find out what the Word says, speak it, and act on it. The more you speak about the problem, the bigger it will get. But the more you hear and speak the Word, the bigger God gets. He gets bigger and bigger and your problem gets smaller and smaller. We serve a mighty God who has exceeding great power. That great power is directed toward us who believe. You need to say, "I'm a believer, not a doubter."

Wouldn't you like to come through a hole in the roof and fall on the head of a Pharisee, who represents educated unbelief? Jesus would love to see it. As Dr. Lilian B. Yeomans commented, "This unlearned, ignorant man almost fell on the reverent heads of the Pharisees."

Maybe you won't come through a hole in the roof, but you can dance and stomp on the foot of the Pharisee next to you. You can also go to church and fall over someone who is trying to figure God out.

All things are possible to the person who believes. That's all you need to know about God - nothing is impossible with Him. God can't be figured out. All we know is that He's a faith God and faith is what pleases Him.

In Luke 5:20, the phrase, "when He saw their faith" should be underlined in your Bible. It refers to the four friends who brought the paralyzed man to Jesus for healing. These men agreed to believe the same thing: Jesus was alive and His anointing and power were present that day to heal. They had real Bible faith, and this kind of faith cannot and will not be denied.

FAITH IS AN ACT:

THE SIMPLEST DEFINITION OF FAITH

IS ACTING LIKE THE BIBLE

IS TRUE.

HEBREWS 11

22

FAITH IS AN ACT
CHAPTER TWENTY TWO

This is the way the Lord explained it to me: faith is an act. Because I'm rather simple sometimes, I pray, "Lord, I just don't understand this, because your thoughts are higher than my thoughts. I don't quite grasp how to get along with You or how to receive from You. I'm not receiving. My 'receiver' is not working right."

Often we think that everyone ought to know how to receive from God. But if that's true, why did Jesus have to spend three and a half years teaching people? People must not have picked it up automatically. Jesus had to teach them how to receive from God. He was always teaching, preaching, and healing.

One thing I appreciate about the teaching ministry of the Lord Jesus Christ is He would say it until you got it. Even if you flunked the third grade and never made it back, Jesus would stick with you until you got it. The only condition was you had to want the help, the blessing, and the miracle.

GET IT BEFORE YOU GET IT

The way things work in the Spirit is that you always have to get it before you'll get it. Some people never get it and that's why they never get it.

Jesus said in Mark 11:24, "What things soever ye desire, when ye pray, believe that ye receive them, and ye shall have them." Another translation says that you believe you've got it, and you'll get it.

You may be thinking, "But I don't have it." That's correct. Jesus said the key was to believe you've received it, and that's when you will get it. When the devil says, "You don't have it," reply, "that's obvious, but I believe I have received it." You'll get it on the inside — in your spirit — before you ever get it on the outside.

THE SPIRIT OF FAITH IS CONTAGIOUS

The principles of faith must be taught, but the spirit of faith must be imparted. We do need teaching, but the spirit of faith must be caught or imparted from someone who already has it. The spirit of faith is contagious.

> *"We having the same spirit of faith, according as it is written, I believed, and therefore have I spoken; we also believe, and therefore speak."*
> - 2 Corinthians 4:13

Notice Paul said, "We have it!" I'm glad he didn't say, "I have it." He was addressing the whole church of Corinth. He was saying that you've got it, I've got it, and you got it from me.

I love to hang around people who have a spirit of faith, people who believe bigger than I can. I'm not intimidated or threatened, but their faith challenges me. God is no respecter of persons; He has no favorites. I know whatever God does for them He can do for me.

Since Jesus instructed us to have faith, it can't be arrogant to say you've got it. Some people might say your being arrogant when you walk in faith. But I imagine the people that hung around Paul thought he was arrogant. Would you have thought that Joshua and Caleb were arrogant? When David killed Goliath and paid to build the temple with an offering of about 1.4 billion people probably thought he was arrogant. In 2 Corinthians 4:13, Paul was quoting David when he said I believed and I spoke.

Obviously David had a spirit of faith. When David was 17 years old, he ran at a giant while everyone else was running away from the giant. To do that, you've got to have a spirit of faith - something no one else has. David's spirit of faith influenced 400 men to join forces with him. When he met these men they were distressed, discontented, and in debt (1 Samuel 22:2). Those three problems usually hang out together. But because of David's spirit of faith they became his mighty men.

FAITH AND FINANCES

David spent much time meditating upon the Word of God and receiving revelation (Psalm 1). He was not simply learning words; he was getting to know the Author who spoke the Words. Many people know Bible verses, but the spirit of faith comes when the Word gets implanted into you. When you get the Word on the inside of you, you get the spirit of faith that comes straight from God. Those 400 men caught the spirit of faith from David, and they became his mighty men (2 Samuel 23:8-23). I believe he taught them about the covenant and about praising and worshiping God. In the Bible you can read about the tremendous things the mighty men did for God and the people of God.

When David brought his offering of $1.4 billion, his mighty men brought their offering of $2.6 billion (1 Chronicles 29:1-9). These dollar amounts are the estimated value of the gold and the silver that was given to build the Temple in Jerusalem.

THE SPIRIT OF FAITH
AFFECTS EVERY AREA

The spirit of faith will invade every area of your life. You can't keep God in one little compartment. The spirit of faith actually affects every area of your life, including your physical health, finances, future, business, and relationships.

As we have seen, the spirit of faith comes not only from feeding on the Word of God, but also from hanging around people who have the spirit of faith. David's mighty men got it, and it affected their finances. Instead of being distressed, discontented, and in debt, they gave an offering of an estimated $2.6 billion!

When it comes to finances, some people have stronger faith in that area than others. There are definitely things that are more important than money, but if you're broke, it's hard to think of them. Psalm 24:1 says, "The earth is the Lord's and the fullness thereof."

God still retains ownership of the earth and God wants you to have things and He wants to bless you for covenant reasons, not for covetous reasons. He gives you power to get wealth to establish His covenant (Deuteronomy 8:18). The spirit of faith is not simply about money, but it does have an effect on your finances.

You ought to be able to get up every morning and say, "I have the God-kind of faith. I have the same kind of faith that created the world in the beginning. I don't have the same measure, but I've got the same kind of faith, and the measure of my faith is increasing."

Smith Wigglesworth said it this way, "Any man may be changed by faith no matter how he may be fettered."

FAITH MUST BE USED

When you learn how to use the God-kind of faith, whatever has bound you must leave. When you have faith you become a target for the devil, so don't be upset when his attacks come. Some people wonder why all hell breaks loose when they get a hold of faith. That's a good time to start laughing, because you know that the devil is trying to get you to renounce your faith. Continue to hold fast to your confession of faith.

Since Jesus said you should have the God-kind of faith, it must be possible to have it. It also must be possible to know that you have it.

If He told you to have it, there will be times in your life when nothing else will work. You've tried everything, professional help of all kinds and nothing worked. But the Holy Spirit is a great Counselor, and the Word of God can get right to the root of the problem. However, you must use your faith.

THE REASON WORDS WILL

MOVE A MOUNTAIN

IS BECAUSE MOUNTAINS

ARE MADE BY WORDS.

23

WHOSOEVER SHALL HAVE WHATSOEVER

CHAPTER TWENTY THREE

"For verily I say unto you, That whosoever shall say unto this mountain, Be thou removed, and be thou cast into the sea; and shall not doubt in his heart, but shall believe that those things which he saith shall come to pass; he shall have whatsoever he saith." - Mark 11:23

In this scripture the word "verily" means, I'm telling you the truth. Jesus said that before He explained exactly how the God-kind of faith works.

I'm so glad the next thing Jesus said was "whosoever." Faith will work for anyone, on any situation, regardless of gender, age, or even education. You don't even have to be smart to have faith. In fact, being smart could be one of your biggest problems. Dr. David Yongi Cho said that God doesn't talk to smart people. He only talks to those who say, "Here I am Lord, teach me something."

The last word emphasized in Mark 11:23 is whatsoever. Whosoever shall have whatsoever. In other words, faith will work for anyone and will work on anything. When I found this out, I started confessing some things rather than just sitting around hoping things worked out. I started charting my course. If faith will work on a mountain, it will work on anything. Sometimes all you need to do is make adjustments in one word or phrase then your faith will work and open you up to the supernatural.

CHECK WHAT YOU HAVE BEEN SAYING

In Mark 11:23 Jesus said, "whosoever...shall have whatsoever he saith." Notice He didn't say, He can have whatsoever. Rather Jesus said, "He shall have...." If you are not happy with what you have in life, you'd better check out what you have been saying. Sometimes it's good to get a faith partner and hold each other accountable for what you are saying.

The God-kind of faith will work on more than one thing at one time. That means you could confess more than one thing at a time. In your struggling, you have been saying, "I need God to do this or that thing." Realize that God can do many things at the same time, and the lights will not even blink in heaven from an overload! God didn't tell you to get your shovel out and move the mountain, He said, "Speak to it." You don't have to struggle, have a nervous breakdown, or a heart attack. Speak to your mountain!

MOTIVATE YOUR FAITH

The Bible also says to fight the good fight of faith. I realize that some people don't have any fight in them. Nevertheless, there is a fight to faith. Either you fight the good fight of faith, or you settle for less than God's best. To possess the land, you'll have to fight for it.

You must be motivated to move your mountain, or you'll make friends with it. You'll hoist a white flag and call a truce. The problem is, when you let a mountain stay there very long, it will attract others, and then you'll have a whole mountain range to deal with.

People get personal about their mountains by saying, "My mountain, my situation." This means they've already drawn it on the map of their life, and they plan on its staying there.

One way the Lord motivated me to speak to my mountain was by saying, "If you knew what was on the other side of your mountain, you would move it. You've been letting that thing stay there for years. The reason that mountain is still there is because the devil is trying to keep you from getting something I have prepared for you."

When you get drunk on the Holy Ghost, the Spirit of God will show you possibilities of what God has ahead for you and cause you to laugh. But after the anointing lifts, you're right back to seeing that mountain, and you say, "My God, I thought that thing was gone."

The Holy Ghost revealed to you the possibility, but you still have to use your faith to move that mountain.

YOU HAVE TO SAY SOMETHING

Genesis 1 says that the Spirit of God moved on the face of the deep, but nothing happened until God said something. The Holy Spirit will move upon you, but nothing is going to change until you say something. You must function with that God-kind of faith. The God-kind of faith will work for anyone and will work on anything.

Jesus said, "You shall have whatsoever you say." Notice, He didn't say that you would have whatsoever is on sale. Some people have a poverty mentality and don't even know it. This is sad because it not only limits their receiving, but it also limits their giving. It limits the blessings God wants to give them.

God wants to do things through you, so take the limits off and let God be God. Jesus didn't say that you would have what others said about you, He said that you have what you say. When you were growing up, your daddy may have called you stupid. Jesus didn't say you're going to have what your daddy said, He said you'd have what you say.

IMPACT THE SEEN AND THE UNSEEN

"And the apostles said unto the Lord, Increase our faith. And the Lord said, If ye had faith as a grain of mustard seed, ye might say unto this sycamine tree, Be thou plucked up by the root, and be thou planted in the sea; and it should obey you."

- Luke 17:5-6

This was not a "deity trick" that worked in heaven alone. Faith will work for whosoever on whatsoever.

"...for verily I say unto you, If ye have faith as a grain of mustard seed, ye shall say unto this mountain, Remove hence to yonder place; and it shall remove; and nothing shall be impossible unto you." - Matthew 17:20

Here, Jesus used a mountain in this scripture to reference our authority over demons and evil spirits. When you speak, your words have an impact not only on the seen but also on the unseen. There are some things I like to say in private just to make sure they have an impact not only on me but also upon the unseen demonic powers.

When I went to Bible college, I used to say certain things about the blessing of the Lord upon my life and future. Friends would come up to me and say, "You'd better not say that, because the devil will hear you." I would answer, "I said it for his benefit. I want to make sure he heard me say it."

RUN UP THE MIDDLE

When I was a little kid, my older brother Mike would get his big friends to play football against me and my little friends. Mike and his team didn't even have a huddle. They would simply walk up to the line and say, "We're going to run straight up the middle and run right over you." And that is exactly what they did.

Once you understand your authority as a believer, you'll be able to say, "Devil, I'm going right up the middle, and I'm running right over you!" Jesus said, "You shall have whatever you say." He didn't say you have what you believe. The spirit of faith must have both ingredients: believing and speaking.

Your mountain needs to hear your voice. Jesus said, "When you speak to the mountain, it will obey you." When Jesus refers to the mountain, He is referring to something that seems too big for you — something that seems impossible. But your mountain will respond to your voice.

MAINTAIN A BOLD CONFESSION

Remember, your individuality is tied up not only in your fingerprints, but also in your voice-print. Your voice-print is a greater definition of your identity than your fingerprint. No other voice-print is exactly like yours. Your voice is your address in the spirit realm. Based upon the authority that He has delegated to you, His power is released when He hears your voice.

I like what the Roman centurion said in Matthew 8. Jesus had told him, "I'll come to your house and heal your servant." The centurion replied, "No, you don't need to come to my house. Speak the Word only, and my servant shall be healed" (verse 8).

Jesus was amazed! He turned to His disciples and said, "I have not found such a great faith in all of Israel" (verse 10). It was almost like He was looking for it. I believe that while Jesus was teaching, He was looking around, thinking, "Let Me see if I can find any faith here."

Remember that before you get to the whatsoever, you must get to the whosoever. Make a bold, daily confession of who you are "in Christ" and what God has done for you through the blood in redemption.

IT TAKES FAITH TO GO

WHERE GOD WANTS YOU TO GO,

AND IT TAKES FAITH TO STAY

WHERE GOD WANTS YOU TO STAY.

24

THE ATMOSPHERE
OF FAITH
CHAPTER TWENTY FOUR

The spirit of faith will charge the atmosphere in your house and your life. If you speak doubt and fear, it will fill the atmosphere with unbelief. But if you speak the Word, you can charge the atmosphere with faith.

I love to eat microwave popcorn. I like to cook it myself because no one else can cook it just the way I do. You have to be talented to cook microwave popcorn.

I get that little bag and put it in the microwave on high. In my microwave, it takes 3 minutes and 45 seconds. While it's cooking, I get things ready in front of the television in the living room. I place a glass of water or maybe a soft drink by my chair and then make sure a good football game is on.

After one minute I check the microwave but nothing is happening yet. The timer is still ticking. After two minutes there is still nothing happening. Then there is a pop, then another pop. The pops come faster and faster; they are multiplied in the last minute until the whole bag is fully popped. The last minute is the most exciting because the pops multiply and the aroma of popcorn fills the house.

While I was observing this process patiently, the Lord spoke to my spirit and said the same thing is true with the promises of God. Sometimes not much happens for a year or two and we think nothing is happening. Then God gives us a sign, a POP. Then another POP! In one year's time God can pop your whole bag of promises and dreams. This is the most exciting time when dreams and promises pop into manifestation!

WHEN NOTHING IS HAPPENING

When you hold fast to your confession of faith, the devil will tell you nothing is happening. It may seem like nothing is happening but that doesn't change anything.

You may have believed God for 30 years, and the devil is telling you that nothing is happening. Continue to hold fast to your confession of faith. I believe that in the next three months, more will happen than has happened in the last 10 or 20 years.

The devil wants you to give up on the God-kind of faith. This is when you need to say, "Hold on a minute! I have a measure of the God-kind of faith. I have a measure of mountain-moving faith. I have overcoming faith. I speak to mountains, and they are removed. And I just heard another pop. Hallelujah."

One time my microwave popcorn went 3 minutes 45 seconds and there were no pops. I was beginning to get really upset. I thought that maybe the microwave had a problem. But when I checked the microwave, someone had changed the setting from high to defrost. If your popcorn isn't popping, you need to check the temperature. You may have been on defrost for the past five years. You need to crank your faith up to high.

GOD'S POWER PUNCH

When you launch out your faith as far as you can, the Holy Spirit shall come upon you and God will give you a power punch. By fighting the good fight of faith and holding fast to a good confession of faith, great things will happen.

God promised in His Word that the mountain would be so far gone that it would be as if it never existed. God said that tumors, cancer, diabetes, high blood pressure, and arthritis will disappear. It will be as though they never afflicted you.

When you speak to strongholds (addictions, attitudes, emotional and mental problems) that have held onto you for years, they will disappear. People will never know that you had that condition unless you tell them. It will seem as though you've always had the victory. You will have to tell them what you did to get rid of it - you spoke to your mountain.

IF YOUR FAITH ISN'T TALKING,

IT ISN'T WORKING.

FAITH ALWAYS HAS A VOICE.

25

THE SPEECH
CENTER EXERCISES
DOMINION
CHAPTER TWENTY FIVE

A leading neurosurgeon has said that the speech center in the brain exercises dominion over the whole central nervous system. He also stated that this is a recent discovery. He said that you can cause different parts of the body to respond with stimuli to corresponding parts of the human brain. However when the speech center is stimulated, the entire central nervous system responds. This means that when anyone says, "I am weak," the speech center sends out the message to the whole body to prepare to be weak. This must be the reason God said,

"Let the weak say, I am strong," -*Joel 3:10.*

BY YOUR WORDS

"For in many things we offend all. If any man offend not in word, the same is a perfect man, and able also to bridle the whole body." - *James 3:2*

Actually, James 3 makes it clear that the tongue controls not only the body, but also the destiny and quality of our lives.

If you could find someone whose speech was perfectly true, you'd have a perfect person, in perfect control of life. A bit in the mouth of a horse controls the whole horse. A small rudder on a huge ship in the hands of a skilled captain sets a course in the face of the strongest winds. A word out of your mouth may seem of no account, but it can accomplish nearly anything — or destroy it! - James 3:2-5, Message

This may seem to be a new discovery in medical science, but the Bible has revealed this fact for thousands of years. Medical science is finally finding out what the Bible says has been true all along.

"For he that will love life, and see good days, let him refrain his tongue from evil, and his lips that they speak no guile." - 1 Peter 3:10

The first thing a doctor does when examining you is look at your tongue. When you go to God with a problem, the first thing He says is, "I see the problem. It's written all over your tongue."

The speech center is the dominion center for our lives. Our words will make us or break us. Our words determine the boundaries of our lives. Our words can limit us or loose us. God gave Adam dominion in the beginning through the power of the spoken word and that has never changed. The Lord Jesus, the Last Adam, said,

"By thy words thou shalt be justified, and by thy words thou shalt be condemned." - Matthew 12:37

Jesus also gave us the classic revelation of how faith works in Mark 11:23 where He said, "Whosoever shall say...he shall have whatsoever he saith." Few people take this revelation as seriously as the Bible emphasizes.

GOD TOUCHES YOUR MOUTH
TO CHANGE YOUR WORLD

Anytime God wants to change someone's life, He touches their mouth. God changes lives through mouth-to-mouth resuscitation. He puts His Words in our mouth to bring life, salvation, and healing.

When God wants to change a city or nation, He always touches someone's mouth. God touched Isaiah's mouth with a coal of fire and sent him to speak words that would change a nation. Those words are still changing lives today — thousands of years later. God touched Jeremiah's mouth and changed his life and a nation. The list of people that God used to change a nation goes on and on, but the most important thing is that right now God is touching your mouth and changing your world.

MAN IS A "SPEAKING SPIRIT"

"And the Lord God formed man of the dust of the ground, and breathed into his nostrils the breath of life; and man became a living soul." - Genesis 2:7

In Genesis 2:7, the phrase, "and man became a living soul," is better translated, "a speaking spirit." God created man in His own image with the capacity to speak and communicate. The power of speech was a major distinguishing factor between the animal kingdom and man. Man was made a speaking spirit and given authority and dominion. Satan recognizes the power of spoken words and is constantly trying to get man to speak words that contaminate, defile and destroy. A constant war is going on for air time. Satan wants to stop the spoken Word of God in your personal life as well as in your city or nation.

YOUR VOICE IS YOUR TICKET OUT OF SATAN'S DOMINION

"Say unto them, As truly as I live, saith the Lord,
as ye have spoken in mine ears, so will I do to you."
- Numbers 14:28

The story of the nation of Israel's failure to possess the Promised Land is clearly described in Numbers 13 and 14. Everyone in these two chapters got exactly what they said. There were twelve spies sent to spy out the land and bring back a report. But two of the spies, Joshua and Caleb, won the war of words when they said, "We are well able to possess the land." Ten of the spies came back and said, "We are not able," and they died in the wilderness.

Words are your address in the spirit realm. Your words custom design and specifically shape your own future. Your speech center exercises dominion in your life.

YOU HAVE BEEN FRAMED

"Through faith we understand that the worlds were framed by the Word of God, so that things which are seen were not made of things which do appear."
- Hebrews 11:3

You often hear these words when working with prison inmates, "I have been framed." The person speaking doesn't realize how true those words really are. The truth is that everyone has been framed. Our words and the words of others have framed our world.

Faith is always made up of the spoken Word of God. F.F. Bosworth said, "It is impossible to boldly claim by faith a blessing that you are not sure God is offering." You cannot boldly possess things you don't realize are available to you. If your confession is wrong, your thinking is wrong, and you will do without God's best blessings.

As we speak the Word of God, it tears down, roots out, builds, and plants (Jeremiah 1:4–12). God wants us to speak His words and frame the picture He has for us. He has a custom plan for each of us in Christ Jesus.

> *"For we are his workmanship, created in Christ Jesus unto good works, which God hath before ordained that we should walk in them."*
> - *Ephesians 2:10*

"LEGO" BIBLE BUILDING BLOCKS

Jesus said in Mark 11:23, "Whosoever shall say...believe those things which he saith...he shall have whatsoever he saith ." He said believe once. He said say, saith, saith three times. Dad Hagin said the Lord told him that he would have to do three times more teaching on the speaking part than on the believing part or people wouldn't get it. The speaking part is vital to faith. Faith is released or put to work by speaking. Again, if you are silent, you lose by default.

In Mark 11:23, Jesus used three different Greek words to explain the speaking part of faith. The first "say" is the Greek word *epo*, which means command. It shows the authority of the believer. The second reference to speaking that Jesus used was the word "saith." This word in the Greek is *laleo*, which means to speak out, use your own voice, and be bold. The third reference to speaking is also the word saith. However this Greek word is *lego* which means a systematic set discourse.

At toy stores we see Lego® sets that contain building blocks for children to construct according to the diagram or picture on the box. Jesus said, "I am giving you a set of Lego® building blocks that you can use to frame your world according to the picture and diagram I have given to you in the Word of God."

The Bible has given us a set of lego building blocks for salvation, healing, blessing, prosperity, and victory in life. Take the Word of God and build by putting His Word in your mouth and framing your future.

"Your success and usefulness in this world will be measured by your confession and your tenacity to hold fast to that confession," F. F. Bosworth. In other words, don't just speak the confession, be tenacious as well. God can be no bigger in you than you can confess Him to be.

A spiritual law that few people recognize is that your situations and circumstances are not what determine your future. Your words and your confessions actually shape and determine what you are and who you will become.

ANY MAN CAN BE CHANGED BY FAITH

NO MATTER HOW

HE MAY BE FETTERED.

-SMITH WIGGLESWORTH

26

GOD'S DAREDEVILS

CHAPTER TWENTY SIX

Every man needs a challenge. Benjamin Franklin challenged lightning and discovered electricity. The Wright brothers challenged gravity and invented the airplane. Man has challenged the heavens and walked on the moon. He has explored the oceans, climbed the highest peaks, ridden river rapids, crossed the deserts, and scorned the Grand Canyon and Niagara Falls.

Recently I stood in the spray and deafening roar of Niagara Falls wondering about the men who had challenged them. I had read of many daredevils who had walked tightropes strung across the foaming jaws of these powerful falls in death-defying feats.

The greatest of these daredevils was a French man named The Great Blondin, a tightrope acrobat who traveled with P.T. Barnum. When Blondin first saw Niagara Falls, excitement pulsed through his veins like a charge of electricity. On July 4, 1859, Blondin walked across a 1,100 foot tightrope over the awesome current. On the same day, he crossed the great falls again. This time enclosed in a sack with only his shackled arms and legs protruding.

Every victory demanded a greater dare. Blondin performed many times before breathless spectators, each time scorning the peril. He ran across the tightrope forward and backward, by day and by night. Blondin even pushed a wheelbarrow across, carrying a small stove. Stopping midway he cooked an omelette, ate part of it, and lowered the rest to the astonished crowd in a boat below!

On August 3, 1859, the Great Blondin, dressed in an Indian costume, mounted the tightrope and crossed the roaring river turning somersaults, suspending himself by one arm and then one leg. He stood on his head on a chair, balancing perfectly above the rushing rapids.

Another time, Blondin crossed the falls on stilts. On August 14, 1859, he asked for a volunteer to ride his back across the tightrope. His manager stepped forward. The Great Blondin strapped the man in a special harness, mounted the harness on his back, and mocked the river again. At the age of 73, Blondin successfully performed his last defiant exploit over the roaring waterfalls.

DEEDS MARKED BY
DARING AND EXCELLENCE

As I stood by the falls getting soaked in the spray, my mind raced over some of the greatest challenges of time and eternity. Blondin's name was special on earth — but was his name written in heaven?

"...The people that do know their God shall be strong, and do exploits," according to Daniel 11:32. Exploits are defined as "deeds marked by daring and excellence."

We can never know our limits or abilities unless they are tested and proven. Within our reach are unlimited possibilities with God. Jesus said in Mark 9:23, "...all things are possible to him that believeth."

I told you the story of our backyard football games, where height and intimidation dominated the outcome. My big brother and his friends would say, "Here's what we're going to do. We dare you to try and stop us!" Their challenge reminds me of David, who announced to Goliath, "I'm going to cut your head off this day," 1 Samuel 17:46.

RISE UP AND DO EXPLOITS

God has challenged the devil throughout the Bible using His daredevils. God always has the strongest and biggest team. He always announces His plans beforehand. From Jesus' birth to His death, to the resurrection, to the outpouring of the Holy Spirit, to the harvest, to the Second Coming of Jesus Christ, God prophesied all His plans ahead of time.

Then He announced, "Devil, I dare you to try to stop Me! I'm running right up the middle!" No devil, no man, and no circumstances can stop God's divine plan for this generation. As God has declared it, we must prophesy and proclaim His power in the earth.

He is Almighty God! He is a mighty Warrior! As we hear and know His voice, new confidence and strength come to us. We will arise with new boldness and declare His dare. It is time for a new generation of men and women to rise up and do great exploits!

THERE ARE THREE KINDS OF PEOPLE:

PIONEERS, SETTLERS,

AND MUSEUM KEEPERS...

27

PIONEERS...
SETTLERS...MUSEUM
KEEPERS

CHAPTER TWENTY SEVEN

On October 14, 1947, Chuck Yeager was the first man to fly 700 miles per hour breaking the sound barrier. For many months, our military had been trying to find a man willing to risk the unknown of supersonic flight. Pilots called it the "ughknown." Some called it the "monster" and said that as soon as the sound barrier was broken, the airplane would disintegrate, and no pilot would survive.

When Chuck Yeager heard of this opportunity he took the challenge. Many unsuccessful attempts were made, and many adjustments were necessary on the plane after each attempt. On the day before his successful flight, Yeager had cracked two ribs in a horseback riding accident. He had to use a sawed-off broom handle to be able to close the hatch on the X-l. His jet was towed up to 40,000 feet by a larger plane and released. As before, his jet took off, headed for 700 mph. No man had been there before. Yeager was determined he would be the first. As he approached 700 mph again, the plane began to rattle and shake, but Yeager was determined and pressed the throttle.

What happened next was spectacular. Observers on the ground heard an explosion, and their hearts sank, thinking Yeager was dead. However, what they heard was a sonic boom. As they watched the sky, the X-l came back into view. Then they realized he had passed the mark. Of course, they had a great celebration.

This was the beginning of America's launch into outer space and NASA's modern space shuttle. Chuck Yeager was a pioneer and became an American hero. The sound barrier everyone else was afraid of had been broken. The way into outer space was opened and many others have followed.

A POKE THROUGH JELL-O

Chuck Yeager said, "The real barrier wasn't in the sky, but in our knowledge and experience of supersonic flight." He described supersonic flight as "a poke through Jell-O" and "sipping lemonade on the front porch."

What barriers do you face as a Christian doing the will of God? The most difficult barriers can be broken and take us to a place in God where we have never been before. What kind of adjustments must be made to break those barriers? Often our own thinking, attitudes, and discipline must be changed to break the barriers. With God's help, the greatest challenges can be "a poke through Jell-O." Then, when the barriers are broken, we can "sip lemonade on the front porch." God has not given us a spirit of fear, but of power, love, and a sound mind (2 Timothy 1:7).

BREAKING BARRIERS

There are always barriers to be broken when we go from glory to glory and from faith to faith. We will experience many breakthroughs in our lives as we overcome the enemy and fulfill all the will of God. David said that the Lord would light his candle, and by Him he could run through a troop and leap over a wall (Psalm 18:28, 29).

I have been to the First Flat-Faced Church where people have tried to leap over the wall and didn't make it. They have a disappointed look on their faces. Their faces are flat because they tried to leap over the wall before they got their candles lit. David knew what it was like to face a challenge. The key is to allow God to light your candle.

"The spirit of man is the candle of the Lord...."
- Proverbs 20:27

When your spirit is lit by God, you can break through every barrier. The spirit of faith is more than just a formula; it is a fire in the spirit of man. The revelation of the Word of God sets your spirit on fire. God's Word is the word of faith, and God is a consuming fire. The Word of God burns in your heart to enable you to overcome in every area of life. That same fire moves you from your comfort zone into greater possibilities and accomplishments.

Some people will never obey God, because they are afraid of the "ughknown." The unknown stops many from moving out into greater blessings in God. The need for security and comfort limits the ability of God to move in their lives. Abraham, on the other hand, left his country and went out into the unknown. According to Hebrews 11:8, "By faith, Abraham, when he was called to go out into a place which he should after receive for an inheritance, obeyed; and he went out, not knowing whither he went." By faith Abraham obeyed God. Faith is obeying God even when there is an element of the unknown. Faith obeys even when you don't feel like it or know all the answers.

"Trust in the Lord with all thine heart; and lean not unto thine own understanding. In all thy ways acknowledge him, and he shall direct thy paths."

- Proverbs 3:5, 6

GOING WHERE YOU HAVE NEVER BEEN

"And they commanded the people, saying, When ye see the ark of the covenant of the Lord your God, and the priests the Levites bearing it, then ye shall remove from your place, and go after it. Yet there shall be a space between you and it, about two thousand cubits by measure: come not near unto it, that ye may know the way by which ye must go: for ye have not passed this way heretofore."

- Joshua 3:3-4

It was necessary for Joshua to have a spirit of faith to lead the nation of Israel out of the wilderness into the Promised Land of Canaan. The people were commanded to move from their place, keep their eyes on the ark, and follow it at a certain distance. They were going into new territory. They had never passed that way before. It seemed that God led them 2,000 cubits at a time.

If God told us everything, we would not have to walk by faith. God wants to take us into new territory. He wants us to go places we have never been and see things we have never seen. It takes a spirit of faith to go into the unknown. The spirit of faith is a pioneer spirit that is not afraid of the unknown.

The spirit of faith will push out from the shore and "...Launch out into the deep...for a draught [catch]...at thy word," Luke 5:4,5.

PIONEERS...SETTLERS...MUSEUM KEEPERS

There are three kinds of people: pioneers, settlers, and museum keepers. Pioneers are continually pressing on into new territory. Settlers stop too soon because they do not care what is beyond the next mountain. They get comfortable and never press on to the possibilities ahead. Some of the tribes of Israel settled too soon and never crossed the Jordan with Joshua. Museum keepers are content to dust off the memories of previous generations and talk about the exploits of the past. However, God has always had a group of pioneers who are willing to take risks and confront the devil.

GOD IS LOOKING FOR PIONEERS -

PEOPLE WHO WILL NOT SETTLE

FOR LESS THAN GOD'S BEST.

28

FAITH TO FORSAKE, FOLLOW, & FORGET

CHAPTER TWENTY EIGHT

A pioneer is defined as "one who ventures into unknown or unclaimed territory; one who opens up new areas; one who prepares the way." There have been and are pioneers today in every field of human experience. We could name the pioneers in science, medicine, transportation, education, technology, and many other fields. There are also pioneers today in the Gospel of Christ — those who are going into new territory and preparing the way for others to follow.

Between 1760 and 1850, America had a massive westward migration. Individuals and whole families loaded covered wagons pulled by oxen, horses, and mules and set out for the unknown. Stories of gold in the mountains, beautiful valleys, and unclaimed territory kept them going. The Santa Fe Trail, the Oregon Trail, the California Trail, and many others were pioneer paths to the future. Daniel Boone, Kit Carson, Davy Crockett, and Lewis and Clark are a few of America's famous pioneers. The pioneers had to know what to take and what to leave behind. Only the most necessary items were allowed. Often the trails were cluttered with things people had to leave behind to make it across the deserts or over the mountains. It was a long journey, and the main rule of every wagon trail was to keep moving. Many people — especially small children, women and the elderly — died along the way, but the pioneers had to keep moving. They always had an expectation about what was ahead.

PIONEERS IN THE GOSPEL

God is always looking for pioneers — people who will not settle for less than God's best. The spirit of faith will keep them moving, and the pioneers will keep expecting miracles. The spirit of faith is not afraid to leave things behind. There are some things that weigh us down and hinder us from making it over the next mountain to the next level of faith and glory. It can be difficult to lay aside treasured items and traditional ways of thinking, but the rewards of obeying God keep us moving.

Hebrews 11:27 says, "By faith, Moses forsook Egypt." It takes faith to forsake the ways of this world and walk in the ways of God. It takes faith to walk away from the pleasures and temptations of this world. Moses did it by faith. Abraham forsook Ur of the Chaldees when he was 75 years old to go to Canaan (Genesis 11:31-12:9). Peter, James, and John forsook their boats and followed Jesus (Mark 1:17,18).

It takes faith to forsake, faith to follow, and faith to forget the past (Hebrews 11:15). If you keep looking back, you can't go forward. That is why God said, "Remember ye not the former things...I will do a new thing; now it shall spring forth...I will even make a way in the wilderness, and rivers in the desert," Isaiah 43:18, 19. In Philippians 3:13-14, the Apostle Paul said, "...forgetting those things which are behind, and reaching forth unto those things which are before, I press toward the mark...."

THE GLORY ROAD

I heard someone prophesy by the Holy Spirit about two roads that lie ahead.

One road goes out ahead and is straight and clear, and you can see what lies ahead, and it looks really nice. That is "The Blessing Road." You can take that road and see the blessing of God in a measure in your life. However, there is another road that goes a different direction up a high mountain. It winds around, and you cannot see what is around the next bend. The mountain looks rugged and rough. When you look at that road, you say, "I sure don't want that road," but that is the road you should take. That is "The Glory Road." There is much sacrifice, and it is much more challenging, but when you get to the top and see what is on the other side, you will be glad you chose that road. The glory of God is to be seen by those who choose this road.

It takes a spirit of faith to choose the glory road. Many just want the blessing and want the road that requires the least effort. God is good and He will bless us as much as He can. There is, however, a choice to make when we want to see the glory of God. The spirit of faith always chooses the glory road.

MOUNTAIN MOVING
AND MOUNTAIN CLIMBING

The spirit of faith moves the mountains that are hindrances to our receiving from God. The spirit of faith also climbs the mountain that represents our obedience to the will of God.

> *"Who shall ascend into the hill of the Lord? Or who shall stand in his holy place? He that hath clean hands, and a pure heart; who hath not lifted up his soul unto vanity, nor sworn deceitfully. He shall receive the blessing from the Lord...."*
> *- Psalm 24:3-5*

> *Who dares climb the mountain of the Lord? – Knox*

The glory road is like climbing the mountain of the Lord. It is like a spiritual Mount Everest. It requires clean hands and a pure heart. It requires training and discipline to make it to the top. However, the rewards at the top make the journey worthwhile. The glory of God can be seen and experienced by those who choose the glory road. A few of the people who have taken it are: David Livingston, Hudson Taylor, Lillian Trasher, P. C. Nelson, William

Seymour, Smith Wigglesworth, Kenneth E. Hagin, Dr. Lilian B. Yeomans, Martin Luther, John Wesley, Lester Sumrall, Aimee Semple McPherson, and many others. In every generation, many choose the glory road to find the divine destiny God has for them. The spirit of faith blazes a pioneer path for others to follow their faith and receive God's best blessings.

WHENEVER YOU BELIEVE GOD,

YOU ALWAYS CHEER UP.

29

THE PIONEER ADVANCE OF THE GOSPEL

CHAPTER TWENTY NINE

The Apostle Paul wrote the letter to the Philippians from prison in Rome. He mentions joy or rejoicing 16 times in four short chapters. Paul was a happy man even in the worst circumstances. He had a spirit of faith. He thanked the believers at Philippi for their partnership in the Gospel. He was not only thanking them, but he was also blessing them with a Word from God that guaranteed every one of their needs met because of their giving (Philippians 4:19).

Another subject that Paul addresses in this letter is the furtherance of the Gospel.

> *"But I would ye should understand, brethren, that*
> *the things which happened unto me have fallen out*
> *rather unto the furtherance of the gospel."*
> *- Philippians 1:12*

The phrase furtherance of the gospel used in this scripture could be translated "the pioneer advance of the Gospel; to go into new territory." Paul was rejoicing about the advance of the Gospel. The Philippian believers were partners with Paul in the pioneer advance of the Gospel. Even though they remained in Philippi, their pioneer spirit of faith was expressed through their giving.

The Gospel of Christ is not meant for a museum - it is for us today. It is full of power and expansion. Settlers put too many limits on the Gospel, because the Gospel is unlimited. We may not see all the results of the spirit of faith during our lifetime. It keeps going, growing, and advancing.

Jesus is the original Pioneer. He is the Author and the Finisher of our faith (Hebrews 12:1, 2). He left Heaven and pioneered the union of God and man. His sacrifice on the cross and His resurrection from the dead joined us to Him through faith.

"And having this confidence, I know that I shall abide and continue with you all for your furtherance and joy of faith." - Philippians 1:25

Believers should continue to advance in the joy of faith. We should go into new areas of joy and believing. The spirit of faith is an ever-increasing faith and an ever-increasing joy.

HISTORY'S HIDDEN TURNING POINT

The spirit of faith is evident in the Apostle Paul's life and ministry. Paul's three missionary journeys were exploits in Christ that changed the world. An article from the April 22, 1991 issue of U.S. News and World Report, by Gerald Parshall, caught my attention.

In the middle years of the first century, preachers of many religions and philosophical stripes traveled the sea lanes and cobblestone roads of the eastern Roman Empire. Among them was an indefatigable evangelist in a rough coat and crude sandals who supported himself in his missionary work by making tents. Contemporary historians did not deem him worthy of a single mention, having no inkling of how great a tent maker Paul of Tarsus was. They could not know that he was erecting the theological tent of Christianity, making it broad enough to accommodate all manner of humankind, to girdle the globe and to survive two millenniums as a major force in history. While Paul traveled by foot, by donkey, by horseback and by boat across Asia Minor and Macedonia establishing new congregations, he reinforced his gospel to previous converts with a series of letters that have awed even secular historians. Will Durant called them "among the most forceful and eloquent...

in all literature."

This article was a part of a larger article entitled *"History's Hidden Turning Points"* by Daniel J. Boorstin, who wrote, "The true watersheds in human affairs are seldom spotted quickly amid the tumult of headlines broadcast on the hour."

The Apostle Paul played a tremendous role in a major turning point in history. The spirit of faith enabled him to obey the "heavenly vision" and change the world. Paul called it "the same spirit of faith." Today, those who follow

Jesus catch the same spirit of faith. We also believe, speak, and establish hidden turning points in people around the world.

THE SPIRIT OF FAITH

WILL MAKE YOU LEAVE

YOUR COMFORT ZONE.

30

SEE YOU AT THE TOP
CHAPTER THIRTY

I recently watched a documentary about Mount Everest and those who have climbed it. As you may know, Mount Everest is the tallest mountain in the world. I was inspired by the challenges of climbing to the top of this mountain. The first men to successfully make it to the top were Sir Edmund Hillary and Tenzing Norgay in 1953. Since then, more than 700 people from around the world have made it to the top of Mount Everest. Many have tried and failed. Others have even lost their lives on the treacherous mountain.

One of the most interesting facts is that climbers cannot go immediately from the bottom to the top. It is physically impossible for the body to adjust to the thin air or the lack of oxygen in a short period of time.

The process of climbing the mountain takes the mountain-climbers from lower camps to higher camps as they gradually make the ascent. Sometimes they stay at high altitude camps for as long as three weeks until their bodies adjust to the high altitude.

During this process, their red blood cells actually double in number to be able to carry enough oxygen to keep them alive. This kind of mountain-climbing must be in your blood in order for you to survive.

In Psalm 24:3-4, God gives a challenge to anyone who wants to move up higher in their fellowship with Him. After He gives the condition of clean hands and a pure heart, He gives the promise of receiving the blessing from the Lord. There are some blessings you cannot receive from God at sea level. You must move up higher in God's presence. As you make adjustments to the altitude, you also make adjustments in your attitude.

The precious blood of Jesus is applied for cleansing and double red blood cells carry much-needed oxygen for you to finish your course. The blood of Jesus provides the double cure for soul and body.

"This is the generation of them that seek him, that seek thy face, O Jacob." - Psalm 24:6

The ascension into God's Holy Place brings you face to face with Jesus. You stand in His presence and are forever changed.

This is a much greater challenge than climbing Mount Everest. The Mountain of the Lord is a much higher calling than the challenges or the achievements of this world.

The true hunger in the heart of every believer is God's presence. This is where satisfaction, fulfillment, and blessings flow. It is time for us to move up higher in the glory of God. The Holy Spirit is our Guide and He will take us to the top if we will listen to Him and follow Him. See you at the top!

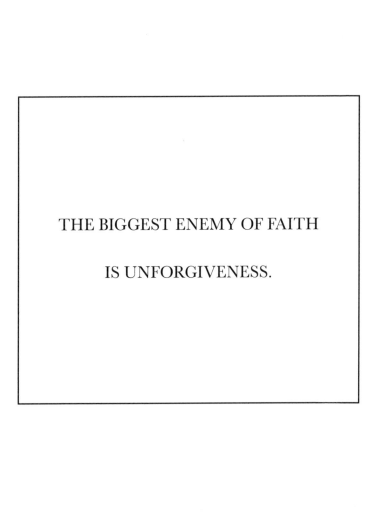

THE BIGGEST ENEMY OF FAITH

IS UNFORGIVENESS.

31

ALL IS FORGIVEN
CHAPTER THIRTY ONE

"I, even I, am he that blotteth out thy transgressions for mine own sake, and will not remember thy sins. Put me in remembrance: let us plead together: declare thou, that thou mayest be justified."
- Isaiah 43:25-26

In Earnest Hemingway's short story, The Capital of the World, he tells the story about a father and his teenage son who lived in Spain. Their relationship became strained, eventually shattered, until the son ran away from home. The father began a long journey in search of his lost and rebellious son. Finally, as a last resort, he put an ad in the Madrid newspaper. His son's name was Paco, a very common name in Spain. The ad simply read, "Dear Paco, meet me in front of the Madrid newspaper office tomorrow at noon. All is forgiven. I love you." The next day at noon, in front of the newspaper office, there were 800 "Pacos" all seeking forgiveness.

COME HOME...BE BLESSED

"I have blotted out, as a thick cloud, thy transgressions, and, as a cloud, thy sins: return unto me; for I have redeemed thee." - Isaiah 44:22

God is in the forgiveness business. Today, many people have trouble accepting the fact that God offers total forgiveness. Psalm 32:1 says, "Blessed is he whose transgression is forgiven, whose sin is covered." The Apostle Paul refers to this verse in Romans 4:6-8. This forgiveness includes the total erasing from His memory that sin was ever committed. He does this for His own sake so He can bless us the way He wants.

When we believe we are forgiven by God Himself, He can bless us as only He can. If God doesn't remember that we have done anything wrong, then we should allow Him to erase it from our memory also. Smith Wigglesworth said, "Never look back if you want the power of God in your life." God's power is always propelling us forward.

NO MORE PARALYSIS

The story of the man with four crazy friends in Luke 5:17-26 is one of my favorites. "When Jesus saw their faith," He told the man with paralysis, "Man, thy sins are forgiven thee." Jesus spoke to that man's deepest need. If Jesus calls you forgiven, you are totally forgiven and released from the condition and consequences of sin. You are redeemed.

Jesus then told the paralyzed man to "Arise!" The man got up totally healed of all paralysis. This miracle caused the religious leaders much trouble. The rules and regulations of religion have paralyzed many people. However, when you get in the presence of Jesus, forgiveness and restoration are freely given. What a wonderful Jesus we have who forgives and heals! He is our Redeemer today.

REMIND ME OF THIS PROMISE

In Isaiah 43:25-26, we know God's promise says that He blots out our transgressions and will not remember our sins. However, we are to put God in remembrance of His Word. God says to remind Him of this promise. This promise of forgiveness and faith in His Word opens the door to God's goodness.

I once heard Dad Hagin say, "Faith will not work in an atmosphere of unforgiveness. If the devil can get you in condemnation – he'll cheat you out of your inheritance." When we receive forgiveness and freely forgive ourselves and others, our faith will work properly. God forgives us so radically and totally, that He commands us to forgive others the same way. God's kind of forgiveness erases the memory of all sin, failure, guilt, and accusation. We plead our case with the Word of God and the blood of Jesus.

"Who forgiveth all thine iniquities; who healeth all thy diseases." - Psalm 103:3

"Who shall lay anything to the charge of God's elect? It is God that justifieth. Who is he that condemneth? It is Christ that died, yea rather, that is risen again, who is even at the right hand of God, who also maketh intercession for us."
- Romans 8:33-34

In 2 Corinthians 5:21, God declares us righteous in Christ. Righteousness is a free gift and those that receive it will reign in life through Christ Jesus (Romans 5:17). This revelation of righteousness makes us glad. These are days of Heaven on Earth, so go ahead and laugh at the devil.

This is the day the Lord has made, so rejoice and be glad. Dare to declare that you are righteous in Christ.

1 Be A People Person , John Maxwell

YOU MAY BE ABLE

TO WHIP A SKUNK, BUT

YOU MIGHT NOT WANT TO!

32

UNFORGIVENESS: THE BIGGEST ENEMY TO FAITH

CHAPTER THIRTY TWO

The greatest hindrance to faith is unforgiveness. This book would not be complete without dealing with this subject.

"Jesus answering saith unto them, Have faith in God. For verily I say unto you, That whosoever shall say unto this mountain, Be thou removed, and be thou cast into the sea; and shall not doubt in his heart, but shall believe that those things which he saith shall come to pass; he shall have whatsoever he saith. Therefore I say unto you, What things

> *soever ye desire, when ye pray, believe that ye receive*
> *them, and ye shall have them." - Mark 11:22-24*

Jesus was talking about faith in verse 22, how to release your faith in your saying in verse 23, and how to release your faith in your praying in verse 24. In the following two verses, He said that the biggest enemy to faith in your life is unforgiveness or offense.

> *"And when ye stand praying, forgive, if ye have*
> *ought against any: that your Father also which is*
> *in heaven may forgive you your trespasses. But if ye*
> *do not forgive, neither will your Father which is in*
> *heaven forgive your trespasses." - Mark 11:25-26*

Notice Jesus said, "...if ye have ought against any." Ought is holding a grudge against someone for any reason. A grudge implies some sort of bitterness. The Bible speaks of a root of bitterness that defiles people (Hebrews 12:15).

Jesus said all things are possible in prayer. However, He pointed out that if you don't deal with unforgiveness, none of your praying, your saying, or your faith will work. Unforgiveness is the door through which the devil enters. He knows that he can neutralize your faith with unforgiveness faster than any other way.

Dad Hagin said it this way, "Anytime you're feeling mistreated, you know that the devil is working on you." If someone really did you wrong, you must forgive them, by releasing them of any unforgiveness on your part. Watch it, because those feelings and that voice of offense will tell you that you've been mistreated. The devil will continue to work on you to set up an offense.

You must not speak against or attack those who have mistreated you. When you release and forgive them, something positive will happen inside you. I like what Smith Wigglesworth said:

> *I realize that God can never bless us on the lines of being hardhearted, critical, or unforgiving. This will hinder faith quicker than anything will. I believe there are a great many people who would be healed, but they are harboring things in their hearts that are as a blight. Let these things go. Forgive and the Lord will forgive you. There are many good people, people that mean well, but they have no power to do anything for God. There is just some little thing that came in their hearts years ago and their faith has been paralyzed since.*

FAITH WORKS BY LOVE

"...faith which worketh by love." - Galatians 5:6

Your faith life will not work properly if you are not walking in love. Faith worketh by love! If your mountain keeps standing there in the same old place, you're not receiving what you're praying for, and your faith is not working — the problem is not with God. The first thing you need to check is your love walk. Evaluate the way you're talking, acting, and conducting your relationships. Walk in love, because faith works by love.

FORGIVENESS IS YOUR RESPONSIBILITY

How long does it take to deal with an offense or unforgiveness? When another person is involved and knows about the problem, the first thing you need to do is say, "I want you to forgive me." You may argue, "What if I tell them I'm sorry, but I feel like it's really their fault, and they won't tell me they're sorry?" Even if that person doesn't reciprocate, it's not your business. Your business is to forgive them. Get rid of that grudge.

However, if the other person doesn't know about the

problem — if it's something you did or something you've been holding against them — there's no reason to get them involved, because you'll stir up more devils than you can cast out. There is no need to tell someone, "I've been mad at you for six months" when they did not know it. Just forgive them and be friendly again.

Ephesians 4:26 says you shouldn't let the sun go down on your wrath. What does that mean? One translation says, "Don't let the sun go down finding you nursing a grudge." This is where the devil has his greatest opportunity to hinder your faith.

Ephesians 4:27 continues, "Neither give place to the devil." If the devil has any place in your life, you gave it to him. You might not have known what you were doing, or you might have given him place through negligence. Negligence means you refused to exercise your authority as a believer. In other words, you refused to do what is right. Another way the devil got in was through disobedience. You knew what the Word said, and you refused to do it. Therefore, you opened the door to the devil.

OLD TESTAMENT EXAMPLES

As you study Job in the Old Testament, you will notice that God turned his captivity when he prayed for his friends

(Job 42:10). Job's friends were really his critics. God can turn your captivity, too, if you will pray for your critics and ask God to bless them.

Joseph is the greatest illustration of God's promotion. He had many opportunities for offense during his life. His brothers cast him into a pit and sold him into slavery. In Egypt, Potiphar's wife falsely accused him of rape and the two men he helped get released from prison refused to speak up for him (Genesis 37, 39, and 40). Joseph could have turned into a bitter, mean, and frustrated man. However, the Bible says that while he was in prison, Joseph willingly did whatever the jailer needed with all of his might. So even while he was in prison, Joseph kept on working as unto the Lord and he never got bitter.

God brought Joseph out of prison, turned the whole situation around, and made him ruler over all of Egypt. Eventually his brothers came to Egypt. They bowed before him begging to buy food in the middle of a severe drought. He could have said, "I've got a chance to get you back now for what you did to me 20 years ago," but he never held that grudge. Instead, he told his brothers, "What you meant for evil God turned for my good. Now I can be a blessing to you."

Joseph was promoted by God, but if he had let unforgiveness and bitterness enter his heart, God could never have taken him where He needed him to go as ruler of Egypt. You need to guard against offenses because they will come. One minister said, "Life is not fair, but God is good."

UNFORGIVENESS CAN CAUSE DISEASE

You may be having to deal with problems that are a result of something someone else did. Keep remembering that God is good and He will bring you out. Remember, unforgiveness is the greatest enemy to your faith, so you must deal with it quickly. We may never find a cure for certain diseases, because all diseases are not simply physical or biological. The devil is the source of it all! When he tricks you into unforgiveness or bitterness, all kinds of incurable diseases may result. Medicine won't be able to cure these diseases, because the cure for them is a matter of the heart - spiritual. When you get things right in your heart you are in position to receive your healing. The cure for certain diseases is forgiveness.

GUARD YOUR HEART

Jesus said, "When you stand praying, forgive." This means, while you are standing praying, you can quickly make an adjustment in your heart. People often let things eat on them for years and years. You can make a decision to forgive. Forgiveness is not a feeling; it's a choice. You may still have feelings of hurt, but you can make a decision to forgive. On the cross, Jesus said, "Father, forgive them." He was telling God to forgive people who had been beating Him, spitting on Him, and mocking Him.

Unforgiveness will get inside you and make your heart callused so your faith won't respond or work properly. Then you will begin to question God's abilities and won't be able to receive from Him. The devil is trying to keep your faith from working and get you to open the door to unforgiveness. If the devil can get in through unforgiveness, sickness will follow and remain. Poverty will also enter and you won't be able to get rid of it. Then the door is open for other problems. This is why you need to close the door of unforgiveness and offense.

Unforgiveness, offense, and bitterness are the primary things you have to guard against. You must watch out for these traps of the enemy just as if they were rattlesnakes.

THE PEACE OF GOD

"Great peace have they which love thy law: and nothing shall offend them." - Psalm 119:165

When you love the Lord, the peace of God is yours and nothing will offend you. The word offense means a place of stumbling — something that trips you up.

The old saying is that to err is human, and to forgive is divine. In other words, we don't live in a perfect world and never will. People will always make mistakes and so will you. So you may as well go ahead and forgive others. Jesus said the amount of forgiveness you dish out is the amount you will get in return (Matthew 7:2). Therefore, you ought to dish out as much forgiveness as you can, because you'll probably need it.

Jesus said in Matthew 7:1, "Judge not, that ye be not judged." Then He said, "Stop criticizing others." Be careful not to judge others when you see them fall. Don't say, "I would never do that." In six months, you may do something worse than that.

Remember, forgiveness is not a feeling; it's a choice! Faith works by love, but the primary enemy of faith is unforgiveness. I encourage you to read 1 Corinthians 13, the great love chapter, every day. Draw the love line out and walk on it.

GOD IS ON MY SIDE,

FOR THE BLOOD HAS BEEN APPLIED.

EVERY NEED SHALL BE SUPPLIED,

& NOTHING SHALL BE DENIED.

SO I ENTER INTO REST,

I KNOW THAT I AM BLESSED.

I HAVE PASSED THE TEST,

I WILL GET GOD'S BEST.

-TRINA HANKINS

33

INSPIRED UTTERANCE

CHAPTER THIRTY THREE

As powerful as the written Word of God is, so also is the prophetic word given under the inspiration of the Holy Spirit. Prophecy is inspired utterance. The simple gift of prophecy is for exhortation, edification, and comfort. Every Spirit-filled believer can and should prophesy. This kind of inspired utterance is a word in season to those who are weary or are facing a challenge.

> *"The Lord God hath given me the tongue of the learned, that I should know how to speak a word in season to him that is weary: he wakeneth morning by morning, he wakeneth mine ear to hear as the learned." - Isaiah 50:4*

FIGHTING WORDS TO WIN THE WAR

"This charge I commit unto thee, son Timothy, according to the prophecies which went before on thee, that thou by them mightiest war a good warfare."

- 1 Timothy 1:18

The Apostle Paul was telling Timothy to remember the prophecies (inspired utterance) concerning him. You need to use such words to win the war concerning your future. Again, the Holy Spirit helps us win the war of words.

"...in accordance with the prophetic utterances which pointed to you." - Revised Standard Version

"...so that you may with their aid put up a splendid fight." - New Berkley Version

"...that being equipped with them you may..."
-Weymouth

"...that inspired by them you may wage the good warfare." - Revised Standard Version

MOUTH TO MOUTH RESUSCITATION

The Holy Spirit gives us God-breathed words that we can speak again and again to help us win. I call this "mouth-to-mouth" resuscitation. When we get words from God's mouth into our mouth, we breathe the life and ability of heaven into our lives. The Word of God was spoken before it was written, and it was written that it might be spoken.

> *"...Man shall not live by bread alone, but by every word that proceedeth from the mouth of God."*
> *- Matthew 4:4*

Many times in my life the Holy Spirit has given me a prophetic word that has made the difference in a battle I was in. We can win every battle with the Word. The Holy Spirit gave this simple prophetic word to my wife, Trina. It is a word in season.

> *God is on my side, For the blood has been applied. Every need shall be supplied, Nothing shall be denied. So I enter into rest, And know that I am blessed. I have passed the test, I will get God's best!*

We have used these prophetic words along with many others to win many battles. The Word of God in our mouth puts the devil on the run. The ammunition is being delivered, so just load up and fire by speaking the Word.

> *"And He hath made my mouth like a sharp sword;*
> *in the shadow of his hand hath he hid me, and*
> *made me a polished shaft; in his quiver hath he hid*
> *me." - Isaiah 49:2*

> *"He made my tongue his sharp sword...."*
> *- New English Bible*

The sword of the Spirit is the Word of God. What a weapon we have in our mouth. When we believe and speak, mountains must move. We have authority as believers. We must win the war of words to win the fight of faith. One General said that in every battle there is a 10-minute span of time that is so crucial, it determines the outcome of the battle. Ten minutes can determine whether you win or lose.

The biggest battle takes place right in our own mouth. Our tongue will determine the outcome of the battles that determine life or death, blessing or cursing, winning or losing. Let's take the written Word of God and the inspired utterances of the Holy Spirit, speak with boldness, and win the war of words. When you run at your giant, speak the Word of God!

THE WORD OF GOD WAS SPOKEN

BEFORE IT WAS WRITTEN,

AND IT WAS WRITTEN

SO IT COULD BE SPOKEN.

34

WORDS

CHAPTER THIRTY FOUR

"Who shall tell thee words, whereby thou and all thy house shall be saved. And as I began to speak, the Holy Ghost fell on them, as on us at the beginning." - Acts 11:14, 15

The Apostle Peter was telling the leaders of the church at Jerusalem about his unusual experience at a Gentile's house. He was quoting Cornelius' experience with the angel who said, "Who shall tell thee words, whereby thou and all thy house shall be saved."

People are saved by hearing words. Words are carriers of salvation. Notice how the Holy Ghost "fell on them" just as in Acts 2. Acts 10:44 says, "While Peter yet spake these words, the Holy Ghost fell on all them which heard the word."

The Holy Ghost fell specifically where people heard the Word. The Spirit of God always lands on the Word. As we speak the Word of God, it opens heaven, and the Holy Spirit falls on us to bring the power of God in this world. These are words that bring salvation, deliverance, healing, blessing, and victory. These are words that move the Holy Spirit of God.

I AM COME FOR THY WORDS

The angel Gabriel, speaking to Daniel, said, "...I am come for thy words," Daniel 10:12. Words not only move God and the Holy Spirit, but angels also respond to words. Here you see angels on assignment going to the place where the right words were spoken. Words of believing prayer and words of faith move Heaven to work on Earth. How important it is for us to understand the power of the spoken word!

THE WELCOMING WORD TO GOD

The word of faith is not such a difficult thing. The

Gospel is called the word of faith in Romans 10:8. The Word is near you. Salvation is near you. Healing is near you. Blessing is near you. How close? It is in your mouth and your heart.

> *"The word that saves us is right here, as near as the tongue in your mouth, as close as the heart in your chest." It's the word of faith that welcomes God to go to work and set things right for us. This is the core of our preaching. Say the welcoming word to God — "Jesus is my Master" — embracing body and soul, God's work of doing in us what He did in raising Jesus from the dead. That's it. You're not "doing" anything; you're simply calling out to God, trusting him to do it for you. That's salvation. With your whole being you embrace God setting things right, and then you say it, right out loud: "God has set everything right between him and me!" - Romans 10:8-10 , Message*

I like that! Say the welcoming word of faith. Acknowledge the Lord Jesus Christ and all He has done for you. Dare to open the door to the supernatural by believing and speaking. God wants to work for you; He just needs you to open the door. Hold fast to your confession of faith. Say it out loud. Win the war of words. God has given us all the ammunition we need.

CONFESSION

ALWAYS PRECEDES AND SUSTAINS

POSSESSION.

35

DAILY CONFESSIONS
OF FAITH

CHAPTER THIRTY FIVE

Make these confessions daily for your faith to grow.

I believe in my heart that God raised Jesus from the dead, and I confess with my mouth that Jesus Christ is Lord. Jesus is my Lord.
- Romans 10:9, 10

I have been born again. God is my very own Father, and I am His very own child. - Romans 8:14, 15

I am a new creature in Christ Jesus. Old things are passed away; behold, all things are new.
- 2 Corinthians 5:17

I can do all things through Christ who strengthens me. - Philippians 4:13

I know I have eternal life. The very life and nature of God is in me. - 1 John 5:11, 12

By the blood of Jesus, I overcome all the works of the devil. - Revelation 12:11

Greater is He that is in me than He that is in the world. - 1 John 4:4

Jesus said He would never leave me nor forsake me, so I can boldly say, "The Lord is my Helper, I will not fear what man can do unto me."
- Hebrews 13:5

It is God who works in me both to will and to do of His good pleasure. - Philippians 2:13

I have been made the righteousness of God in Christ Jesus. - 2 Corinthians 5:21

My God supplies all my needs according to His riches in glory by Christ Jesus. - Philippians 4:19

The Lord is my shepherd. I shall not want or lack for anything. - Psalm 23:1

The Lord is the strength of my life. I am strong in the Lord. - Psalm 27:1

About the Author

Mark and Trina Hankins travel nationally and internationally preaching the Word of God with the power of the Holy Spirit. Their message centers on the spirit of faith, who the believer is in Christ, and the work of the Holy Spirit.

After over 40 years of pastoral and traveling ministry, Mark and Trina are now ministering full-time in campmeetings, leadership conferences, and church services around the world and across the United States. Their son, Aaron and his wife Errin Cody, are now the pastors of Christian Worship Center in Alexandria, Louisiana. Their daughter, Alicia Moran and her husband Caleb, pastor Metro Life Church in Lafayette, Louisiana. Mark and Trina also have eight grandchildren.

Mark is also the author of several books. For more information on Mark Hankins Ministries, please log on to our website, www.markhankins.org.

Mark Hankins Ministries

PO BOX 12863 ALEXANDRIA, LA 71315

Phone: 318.767.2001 E-mail: contact@markhankins.org

Visit us on the web: www.markhankins.org

Mark Hankins Ministries
Publications

SPIRIT-FILLED SCRIPTURE STUDY GUIDE

A comprehensive study of scriptures in over 120 different translations on topics such as: Redemption, Faith, Finances, Prayer and many more.

THE BLOODLINE OF A CHAMPION - THE POWER OF THE BLOOD OF JESUS

The blood of Jesus is the liquid language of love that flows from the heart of God & gives us hope in all circumstances. In this book, you will clearly see what the blood has done FOR US but also what the blood has done IN US as believers.

TAKING YOUR PLACE IN CHRIST

Many Christians talk about what they are trying to be and what they are going to be. This book is about who you are NOW as believers in Christ.

PAUL'S SYSTEM OF TRUTH

Paul's System of Truth reveals man's redemption in Christ, the reality of what happened from the cross to the throne and how it is applied for victory in life through Jesus Christ.

THE SECRET POWER OF JOY

If you only knew what happens in the Spirit when you rejoice, you would rejoice everyday. Joy is one of the great secrets of faith. This book will show you the importance of the joy of the Lord in a believer's life.

11:23 – THE LANGUAGE OF FAITH

Never under-estimate the power of one voice. Over 100 inspirational, mountain-moving quotes to "stir up" the spirit of faith in you.

LET THE GOOD TIMES ROLL

This book focuses on the five key factors to heaven on earth: The Holy Spirit, Glory, Faith, Joy, and Redemption. The Holy Spirit is a genius. If you will listen to Him, He will make you look smart.

THE POWER OF IDENTIFICATION WITH CHRIST

Learn how God identified us with Christ in His death, burial, resurrection, and seating in Heaven. The same identical life, victory, joy, and blessings that are In Christ are now in you. This is the glory and the mystery of Christianity – the power of the believer's identification with Christ.

REVOLUTIONARY REVELATION

This book provides excellent insight on how the spirit of wisdom and revelation is mandatory for believers to access their call, inheritance, and authority in Christ.

GOD'S HEALING WORD by Trina Hankins

Trina's testimony and a practical guide to receiving healing through meditating on the Word of God. This guide includes: testimonies, practical teaching, Scriptures & confessions, and a CD with Scriptures & confessions (read by Mark Hankins).

Acknowledgments

Special Thanks to my wife, Trina.

My son, Aaron and his wife, Errin Cody their daughters, Avery Jane and Macy Claire, their son, Jude Aaron.

My daughter, Alicia and her husband, Caleb their sons, Jaiden Mark, Gavin Luke, Landon James, and Dylan Paul, their daughter Hadley Marie.

My parents, Pastor B.B. and Velma Hankins, who are now in Heaven with the Lord.

My wife's parents, Rev. William and Ginger Behrman.

BE SURE TO DOWNLOAD
—— THE ——
Mark Hankins Ministries
MOBILE APP
AVAILABLE IN THE APP STORE & ON GOOGLE PLAY

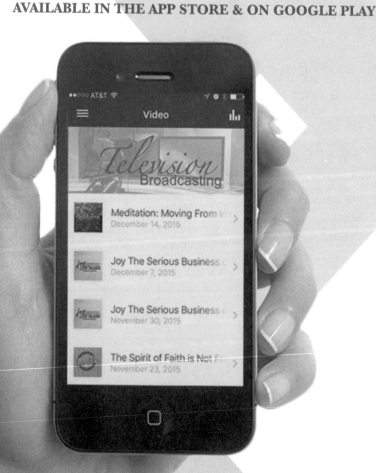

TAKE YOUR FAITH DEEPER!

icibc

IN CHRIST INTERNATIONAL BIBLE COLLEGE

Sign up today for the
MHM Correspondence Bible School
18 Month Accredited
Training Program

For more information, visit us at www.markhankins.org
or call us at 318.767.2001

Notes

Notes

Notes

References

Amplified Bible. Zondervan Publishing House, Grand Rapids, Michigan, 1972.

Boorstin, Daniel. "History's Hidden Turning Points," US News and World Report, 22 April, 1991: 52.

Bosworth, F.F. Christ The Healer. Fleming H. Revell, Grand Rapids, MI, 2005.

Cartmill, Matt. "The Gift of Gab," Discover Magazine, Nov: 1998: 56.

Frankl, Viktor. Man's Search for Meaning. Washington Square Press, New York, New York, 1984.

Gossett, Don and Kenyon, E.W. The Power of Your Words. Don and Joyce Gossett, Blaine, WA, 1977.

Heflin, Ruth Ward. Glory. The McDougal Publishing
Company, Hagerstown, MD, 1990.

Jordan, Clarence. The Cotton Patch Version of Paul's
Epistles. Association Press, New York, New York, 1968.

Kenyon, E.W. The Two Kinds of Life. Kenyon's
Publishing Society, 1997.

Knox, Ronald. The Shorter Knox Bible. Macmillan and
Company Unlimited, London, England, 1958.

Lemonick, Michael. "What's Hiding in the Quark,"
Time magazine, 19 Feb. 1996: 54.

Maxwell, John. Be a People Person. Victor Books, a
division of Scripture Press Publication Inc, US, Canada,
England, 1989.

New English Bible. Oxford University Press, Oxford,
England, 1961.

Parshall, Gerald. The Momentous Mission of the Apostle Paul," US News and World Report, 22 April, 1991: 54-55.

Peterson, Eugene. The Message/Remix, The Bible in Contemporary Language. NavPress Publishing Group, Colorado Springs, Colorado, 2003.

Revised Standard Version. Thomas Nelson and Sons, New York, New York, 1952.

Rotherham, J.B. The Emphasized Bible. Kregel Publications, Grand Rapids, Michigan, 1976.

The Bible in Basic English. University Press, Cambridge, England, 1965.

The Jerusalem Bible. Double Day and Company, Inc. New York, New York, 1968.

Verkuyl, Gerrit. The Holy Bible, The New Berkeley Version Revised Edition in Modern English. Zondervan Publishing House, Grand Rapids, Michigan, 1969.

Webster, Noah. The American Dictionary of the English Language, 1828. www.cbtministries.org/resources/webster1828.htm

Weymouth, Richard Francis. The New Testament. James Clark and Company, London, England, 1909.

Wigglesworth, Smith. Ever Increasing Faith. Gospel Publishing House, Springfield, Missouri, 1971

Yeager, Chuck and Leo Janos, Yeager. Bantam Books, New York, New York, 1985.

Yeomans, Lilian. The Great Physician. Gospel Publishing House, Springfield, MO, 1933.